An A-to-Z Tour of England

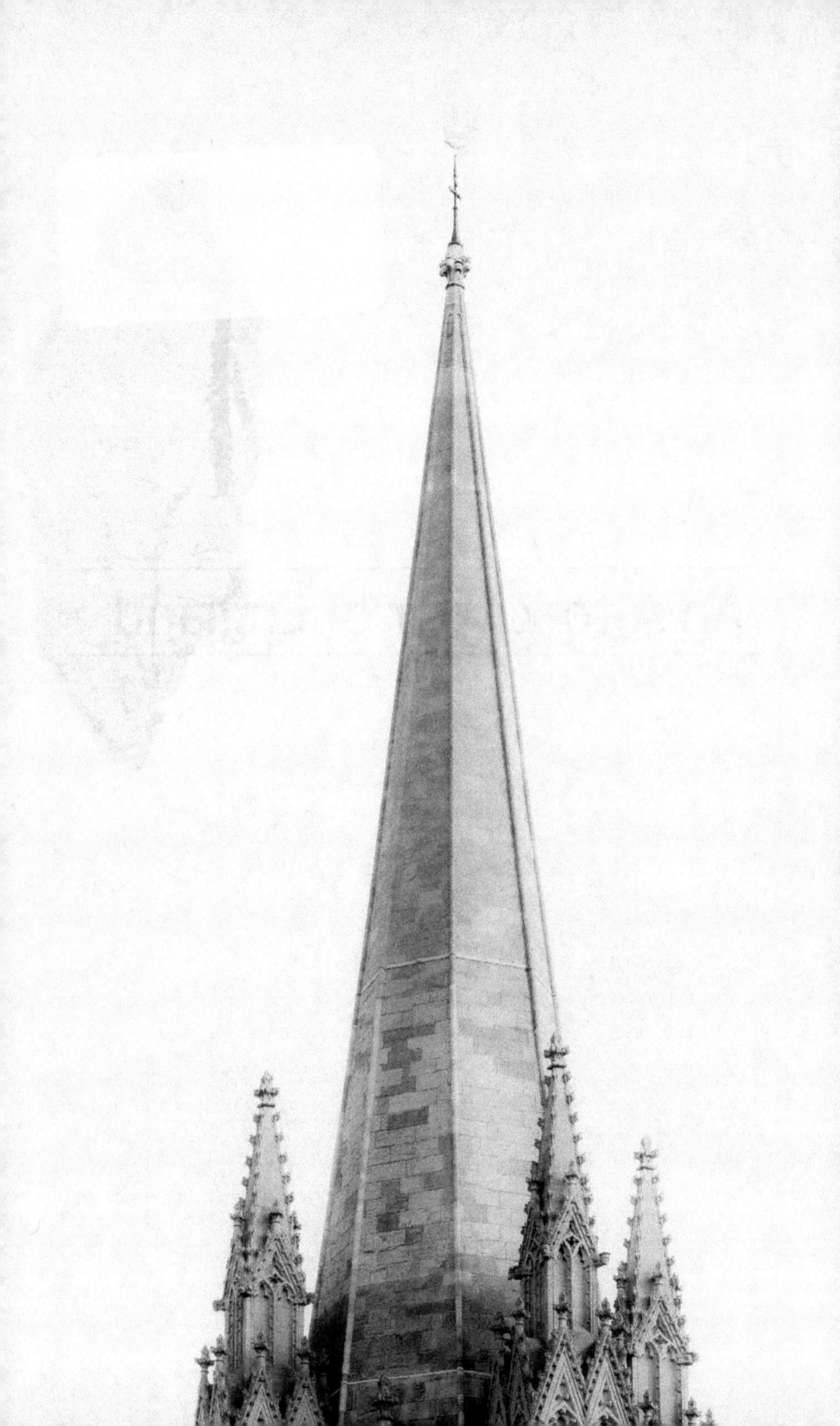

An A-to-Z Tour of England

Using Public Transport

by

Martin Miller-Yianni

Publisher: M P Miller-Yianni, Yambol, Bulgaria.

Published: 2023 (1st Edition)

ISBN 978-619-7742-04-6 (paperback)

A catalogue record for this book is available from:

The National Register of Published Books in Bulgaria
bulevard 'Vasil Levski' 88,
1504 Sofia,
Bulgaria

Credits:

Cover photograph by Matthew Waring from Unsplash.com
Internal Photographs from Unsplash.com and Wikipedia.com

Introduction

It's spring 2019 and I yearn for change, something that will inject much-needed excitement into my existence. Suddenly, like a revelation, it hits me—I need an adventure! But not just any ordinary adventure. I crave something outlandish, wild, and utterly crazy. That's when an idea forms in my mind—why not embark on an A-to-Z tour of England?

Picture this: I'll travel across the country, visiting towns, cities, and villages in alphabetical order. It will be like a treasure hunt, seeking out hidden gems that are quirky and charming, scattered all over the land.

To make it even more exhilarating, I decide to rely solely on public transport. Buses, trains, trams—I'm ready to tackle them all! I want to fully immerse myself in the local culture, interact with people, and observe life unfolding around me like a curious and excited observer.

Armed with an open mind and a backpack filled with essentials, I set off on my alphabetical escapade. From Amersham to Zouch, each day promises a new surprise. There will be magnificent castles, tea-sipping old ladies, and mystical stone circles.

I have allotted just one day for each place, which means my schedule will be packed tighter than a suitcase bursting with souvenirs. I'll indulge in local delicacies, marvel at stunning architecture like towering cathedrals and wonky old cottages, and eagerly dive into whatever adventure awaits me around the next cobbled street.

However, it's not just the destinations that will make this adventure truly magical—it's the people I meet along the way. I can't help but smile at the audacity of my grand plan. Who knew that a simple alphabetical tour could turn into a whirlwind of laughter, discovery, and unforgettable moments? So, I am all set for my epic A-to-Z Tour of England, and here's what I've packed to make it a breeze:

First and foremost, my trusty rucksack is loaded with the essentials. I've packed the absolute minimum of clothing—just enough to get by. It's important to stay light on my feet, you know? I've also made sure to grab travel-sized toiletries like toothpaste, shampoo, conditioner, and all the necessary bathroom goodies. Staying fresh on the road is crucial!

With my phone in hand, I have navigation covered, and I even have an old-fashioned map of England as a backup. No need to worry about getting lost in the English countryside. Plus, it's great for staying connected with friends and family along the way. I can't forget the chargers, though—I don't want my phone to die on me when I need it the most!

Money matters, right? So, I have my credit and debit cards at the ready. I want to be prepared for any financial situation that arises. I've ensured they're all valid, and I've informed my bank about my travel plans. And hey, a bit of cash always comes in handy too, just in case I stumble upon a charming little village that operates on a cash-only basis.

Time management is crucial for this adventure. If I have a far-off destination, there's no hitting that snooze button! I'll be up and ready before the birds even start chirping. I want to allow ample time to reach my target before midday. I've done some research as well, checking out traffic conditions and possible delays. I want to be prepared for anything!

So, there you have it! With my rucksack, smartphone, cards, map, and an early start, I'm ready to conquer this A-to-Z Tour of England. It's going to be a thrilling experience exploring this beautiful country, one destination at a time.

Let the adventure begin!

TABLE OF CONTENTS

AMERSHAM THE FIRST CALL

Having arrived from Bulgaria the day before, I woke up and found myself in a simple bed and breakfast accommodation in the delightful town of Amersham, nestled away in Buckinghamshire. Its enchanting allure quickly whisked me away, as if I had stumbled upon a hidden gem patiently waiting for me to discover its wonders.

My first stop on this tour was the Amersham Museum, a treasure trove of history and nostalgia. I delved into its exhibits with wide-eyed curiosity, immersing myself in the tales of the town's medieval beginnings and its vibrant arts and crafts scene. It felt like stepping back in time with a museum ticket—a crash course in Amersham's culture that left me in awe of its rich heritage.

With a newfound appreciation for the past, I ventured into the heart of the old town. The cobbled streets beckoned me to wander through a whimsical maze of timber-framed buildings, each one oozing with charm. Market Square buzzed with life, as locals and visitors mingled among independent shops, tantalising cafes, and eateries that seemed plucked straight from a fairy-tale. The scent of freshly brewed coffee and baked goods wafted through the air, casting a spell on my taste buds. How could I resist the allure of a classic afternoon tea? Indulging in delicate sandwiches, warm scones slathered with clotted cream and jam, and a comforting pot of tea, I embraced the British tradition with gusto and a few crumbs to spare.

Seeking solace in nature's embrace, I meandered towards the Amersham Commons—a green haven nestled amidst the town's hustle and bustle. The serenity of the place washed over me like a gentle breeze, soothing my soul. Strolling along tranquil paths, I marvelled at the vibrant flora and took in sweeping vistas of the Chiltern Hills. The sweet birdsong and rustling leaves provided a soothing soundtrack, harmonising with the rhythm of my heart.

Eager to broaden my horizons, I embarked on a short journey to the Chiltern Open Air Museum. This living museum unfolded like a time capsule, housing historic buildings that whispered tales of bygone eras. I wandered through thatched cottages, stepped into the shoes of Victorian residents in a farmhouse, and let my imagination run wild in the halls of a medieval barn. Each structure held secrets and stories that stirred my imagination, immersing me in the region's architectural legacy.

As the sun began its descent, I didn't want to stay in the same place as the night before and sought refuge in a cosy, 3-star hotel called The Saracens Head which is 1.4 km from the centre of Amersham. With its inviting ambiance and convenient location, it was a home away from home—a sanctuary to rest my weary feet.

The evening's menu at the hotel's restaurant was a culinary delight. I began with the Crispy Sussex Brie with Red Onion Marmalade, relishing the warm, gooey brie enclosed in a crispy golden crust. For the main course, I opted for the Pan-Seared Cotswold Lamb with Minted Pea Puree—a superb dish showcasing tender lamb accompanied by vibrant green pea puree. The flavours were harmonious and thoroughly satisfying. The meal was a true indulgence, highlighting the chef's expertise and the culinary treasures of the region.

The warmth of the staff and the cosy atmosphere wrapped around me like a comforting hug, leaving me content and eagerly anticipating the next leg of my adventure early the following morning.

No smoking
Way out →
AMERSHAM

AMERSHAM TO BATH

Right-o, time to get the ball rolling in jolly old Amersham! I make my way to the Amersham Underground Station, greeted by those iconic red and blue signs that scream "London, here we come!" The station is buzzing with eager commuters, all raring to go on their morning adventures. I hop on the Metropolitan Line train and off we go, whizzing through the lush greenery of Buckinghamshire.

As I peer out the train window, I'm treated to a real sight for sore eyes. The English countryside unfolds before me like a picture postcard. Rolling hills, charming villages, and vast fields stretch out as far as the eye can see. It's like being in the middle of a proper British painting. The train makes its stops at these cute little stations, giving us a taste of local life in these small towns.

After about 40-50 minutes, we finally arrive at the bustling Baker Street Underground Station. Stepping off the train, I'm greeted by a lively crowd of Londoners and tourists, all buzzing around like busy bees. It's a proper hustle and bustle! I make my way through the maze of tunnels and before I know it, I'm at the magnificent Marylebone Station, feeling like a real VIP with its fancy architecture.

Inside the station, it's like a vibrant register of people from all walks of life. You've got sharp-suited business folks, families with excited kiddos, and wide-eyed tourists clutching their maps for dear life. It's a right ol' melting pot of characters, and I can't help but get caught up in the electric atmosphere.

Finding a comfy seat on the train departing from Marylebone, I settle in for the next part of the adventure. As we move away, the concrete jungle starts to fade away, making room for open fields and peaceful rivers. The scenery changes as we head further west, passing through these charming towns and villages that look straight out of a storybook.

I spy quaint cottages, historic buildings, and gardens bursting with colours. It's like a real-life watercolour! And through the train window, I catch glimpses of the locals going about their business, giving me a cheeky peek into their world.

And then, Bath Spa Station comes into view, and I can hardly contain my excitement. The train snakes along the Avon Valley, treating me to jaw-dropping views of lush green hills and a meandering river. I can practically feel the magic of Bath in the air, even before I set foot in the city.

Finally, the moment arrives, and I jump off the train, greeted by the stunning architecture and Georgian elegance that defines Bath. I leave the station behind and dive headfirst into exploring all that Bath has to offer. First stop, the Roman Baths—a proper UNESCO World Heritage site. Those ancient ruins and fascinating history have me gobsmacked.

Next up, Bath Abbey towers above the city, with its stunning Gothic architecture making me go, "Blimey, that's impressive!" And you can't miss the Royal Crescent, a row of posh Georgian townhouses that just screams "fancy!" The city is teeming with charm and beauty.

As I wander the lively streets, I stumble upon quirky shops, cosy cafes, and friendly pubs. The famous Bath stone buildings, with their warm honey-coloured facades, add to the city's undeniable charm. I can't resist soaking in the famous thermal spas, pampering myself in those warm, mineral-rich waters. It's pure bliss, a proper treat for the senses.

As the day winds down, I find myself sporting a broad grin as I look back on my time in Bath. It's been an absolute cracker of a day, and now I make my way back to Bath Spa Station. Reflecting on the journey, I can't help but feel ever so grateful for experiencing the fantastic transition from the enchanting town of Amersham to the vibrant and historic city of Bath. It's been a right proper adventure, and I can't wait to see what's in store next on this merry tour of jolly ol' England!

With a touch of tiredness in my stride, I approach Bath Spa Station, passing by The Z Hotel Bath, a delightful 2-star accommodation situated a mere 350 metres from the bustling centre of Bath. Having spent the night there, I can't help but appreciate the hotel's convenient location, which allowed me to easily immerse myself in the city's vibrant atmosphere. The Z Hotel Bath may not have boasted extravagant luxuries, but it more than made up for it with its cosy and inviting ambience.

As I wearily entered the hotel, I was greeted by a warmly lit lobby adorned with tasteful décor, creating a welcoming and pleasant environment. The friendly receptionist wore a beaming smile and provided impeccable assistance throughout my stay, making me feel truly at home. Though the hotel may have been modest in its offerings, it provided all the necessary amenities for a comfortable and restful experience.

My room, though compact, was cleverly designed to maximise space without compromising on comfort. The snug bed embraced me in its softness, guaranteeing a peaceful night's sleep. The modern en-suite bathroom boasted clean lines and invigorating shower facilities, offering a refreshing start to the day.

BATH TO CAMBRIDGE

Off I jolly well went from the splendid city of Bath, all set for a ripping good adventure to the prestigious city of Cambridge. I stepped up on some top-notch public transport, making sure my journey was as smooth as a cucumber sandwich. Little did I know that the trip itself would be an absolute corker, with loads of captivating sights along the way.

First things first, I boarded a train at Bath Spa station and found myself surrounded by the most picturesque English countryside. The train whisked me through the rolling hills of Somerset and Wiltshire, and let me tell you, the view was absolutely splendid. I couldn't help but feel a sense of peace as I gazed out at the quaint villages and lush farmlands whizzing by.

Next stop, Swindon! Now, this place is known for its rich railway heritage, so I couldn't resist taking a moment to soak in the sights of the famous Swindon Railway Works. It's a proper testament to the town's industrial past, I tell you. And let's not forget about the Swindon Museum and Art Gallery, brimming with fascinating exhibitions that give you a real taste of the area's vibrant culture.

After a short jaunt, I arrived at London Paddington station, where it was time to switch things up and catch a good old' London Underground. Boarding the Tube, I joined the Circle Line and let the buzzing energy of the city envelop me as we zoomed through those underground tunnels. I caught fleeting glimpses of London's famous landmarks, like the majestic St. Paul's Cathedral and the bustling Covent Garden, before they disappeared in the blink of an eye.

Well, fancy that! I arrived at London King's Cross station, and let me tell you, it's a sight to behold. The grand architecture of the station had me gobsmacked. I took a moment to soak in the impressive facade and the hustle and bustle of the concourse. The excitement for the next leg of my journey was bubbling up inside me like a freshly brewed cuppa.

From King's Cross, got on a direct train to Cambridge. As we sped northeast, the landscape transformed into a picturesque painting of fenlands and meandering rivers. I couldn't help but stare out at the serene beauty, with the clear blue sky reflected in the calm waters below. It was like a dream, I tell you.

Finally, I arrived in Cambridge, and it was like stepping into a world of rich history and intellectual wonder. The architecture of Cambridge University, with its grand spires and imposing college buildings, called out to be explored. The famous King's College, with its jaw-dropping chapel, left me utterly gobsmacked. I couldn't believe I was standing in front of such an architectural masterpiece.

As I strolled along the cobbled streets, I found myself by the tranquil River Cam, where punts gracefully glided through the water. The peaceful ambiance and the lush college gardens offered a perfect escape from the hustle and bustle of the city. Of course, I couldn't resist taking a punt ride myself, enjoying the majestic views of the colleges and bridges as I glided along the river.

And what's a visit to Cambridge without indulging in a proper afternoon tea? I found myself in a charming tea room, tucking into delicate sandwiches, freshly baked scones with clotted cream and jam, and a fragrant cuppa. It was pure bliss, a moment of utter relaxation in the heart of the city.

As the day turned to night, I decided to extend my stay in Cambridge and soak up its lively nightlife. I ventured out into the bustling streets, where a plethora of restaurants, bars, and entertainment venues awaited. I opted for a restaurant randomly picked, where I treated myself to a culinary masterpiece. I started with Cambridge Crab Cakes, a delightful blend of tender crab meat with a crispy exterior. For the main course, I savoured a perfectly pan-seared Suffolk Beef Fillet, accompanied by roasted vegetables and sautéed wild mushrooms. The sommelier expertly paired each course with exquisite wines. To end on a sweet note, I indulged in a warm Sticky Toffee Pudding with toffee sauce and vanilla ice cream. It was a memorable dining experience that showcased Cambridge's vibrant food scene.

After a satisfying meal, I took a leisurely stroll through the beautifully illuminated streets of Cambridge. The soft glow of the streetlights cast a magical spell over the city's iconic landmarks, like the awe-inspiring King's College Chapel and the picturesque Trinity College. I couldn't help but soak in the rich history and tradition as I walked in the footsteps of countless scholars.

As the day draws to a close, I eagerly make my way back to my lodgings for the night, The Union Suite, located just a stone's throw away—600 meters, to be precise—from the bustling centre of Cambridge. Let me tell you, stepping into this place felt like stepping into a world of pure luxury and indulgence. They certainly know how to treat a person like a proper VIP!

From the moment I set foot in the door, it was clear that they had thought of every little detail. It was like entering a haven of ultimate comfort and relaxation. The room? Oh, it was pure heaven. The bedding was so plush and inviting, I practically sank into it like a marshmallow. The ambiance? Utterly serene and tranquil, making me feel like I had my own personal oasis.

And let's not forget about the fancy amenities! They had it all covered, my dear chap. It was like having my own personal spa retreat right there in the room. I may have spent a bit too much time basking in the luxurious shower, enjoying every moment of being pampered like a true royal.

With such a perfect setup, you can bet your bottom penny that I had the jolliest good night's sleep. It was like drifting off to dreamland on a cloud of pure bliss. And let me tell you, waking up refreshed and ready to conquer another day of marvellous exploration and thrilling discoveries was an absolute treat.

So, here's to The Union Suite, my posh sanctuary in the heart of Cambridge. They certainly know how to make a person feel like the cat's whiskers.

CAMBRIDGE TO DURHAM

Time to bid a jolly cheerio to the enchanting city of Cambridge and embark on the next leg of my A-to-Z adventure through England. This time, I set my sights on the historic city of Durham, relying on public transport to whisk me away on this thrilling escapade. Little did I know that the journey itself would be filled with splendid experiences and captivating sights.

With a quick step, I got aboard a train at Cambridge Station, brimming with excitement for the adventure that awaited. The train forced its way northwards, revealing rolling hills and quaint villages along the way. It was a serene and idyllic backdrop for my delightful voyage.

We made a quick stop at Peterborough Station, offering a momentary pause before continuing our jaunt to Durham. The station's splendid architecture, with its grand entrance and intricate details, spoke volumes about its historical significance and the importance of rail travel in connecting communities.

Back on the train, I settled into my seat and gazed out of the window, eagerly awaiting the ever-changing vistas. As we ventured further into the North East, the landscape underwent a magical transformation. Rugged moorland and vast open spaces unfolded before my eyes, painting a breathtaking panorama. The train meandered through tunnels and over viaducts, treating me to magnificent views of the surrounding countryside.

The charm of the small towns and villages we passed along the way was utterly captivating. Each one had its own unique character, with charming stone cottages nestled among green fields and bustling marketplaces where locals gathered to trade and have a good old chinwag.

At long last, we arrived at Durham Station, and as I disembarked, I was filled with eager anticipation to explore this historic city. Making my way towards the city centre, I was immediately greeted by the sight of the magnificent Durham Cathedral, proudly perched atop a hill, demanding attention. Its intricate stonework and soaring spires were a testament to the skill and craftsmanship of the builders who brought it to life.

Meandering through the winding medieval streets, I stumbled upon hidden nooks and charming corners, each one revealing a slice of Durham's rich heritage. The cobbled paths led me to the stunning Durham Castle, majestically sitting on a hill overlooking the River Wear. Its imposing presence and well-preserved Norman architecture served as a reminder of its centuries-old history and the pivotal role it played in the region.

I simply couldn't resist the allure of the riverbanks, where the serene River Wear meandered through the city. Crossing over the iconic Prebends Bridge, I paused to take in the breathtaking views of the cathedral and castle, their reflections shimmering in the water. The tranquillity of the scene offered a moment of respite and reflection.

Immersing myself in the city's vibrant culture, I paid a visit to the charming shops, lively markets, and inviting cafes that lined the streets. The tantalizing aroma of freshly brewed coffee wafted through the air, while the friendly banter of locals created a lively and convivial atmosphere. I couldn't resist indulging in some traditional delicacies, such as the renowned Durham oatcakes, or treating myself to a hearty pub lunch accompanied by a pint of local ale, fully immersing myself in the region's rich culinary traditions.

As the day drew to a close, I found myself reflecting on the experiences I had encountered during this leg of my journey. The captivating landscapes, awe-inspiring architecture, and warm hospitality of

Durham had left an indelible impression on me. It was a city that effortlessly combined its rich history with a vibrant present, beckoning visitors to explore and uncover its hidden treasures.

I found myself staying at the delightful Castle View Guesthouse, a mere 550 meters from the bustling centre of Durham. Let me tell you, this place had "cosy" written all over it in big, friendly letters.

As I stepped into the guesthouse, it welcomed me like an old friend. The atmosphere was simply splendid, with a charming blend of homely comforts and warm hospitality. You could feel the love and care that went into every little detail.

The room was like a snug little sanctuary, designed for a blissful snooze. I nestled into the sumptuous bedding, feeling as snug as a bug in a rug. The peaceful surroundings guaranteed a night of restful slumber and rejuvenation.

So, there I was, drifting off into dreamland, ready for the next chapter of my adventure. Castle View Guesthouse may not have been a grand castle itself, but it offered a warm and inviting haven. With every passing day, I discovered more of its captivating wonders.

DURHAM TO ECCLES

Waking up fully refreshed, I find myself eagerly anticipating the exciting sights and experiences that lie ahead. Armed with a sense of adventure, I embark on this delightful narrative, ready to jot down the intriguing moments along the way.

My grand journey begins at the lively Durham Railway Station, bustling with commuters and fellow travellers. After getting my ticket, I board a train bound for Manchester Piccadilly Station. Settling into a cosy seat by the window, I prepare myself for a scenic ride, eager to witness the ever-changing landscapes.

As the train bids farewell to Durham, the picturesque countryside unfolds like a dream. Rolling hills, quaint villages, and verdant green fields pass by, creating a serene and enchanting backdrop for my journey. I can't help but be captivated by the natural beauty that surrounds me.

The train journey from Durham to Manchester takes a couple of pleasant hours, but time seems to fly by as I become fully engrossed in the captivating scenes outside. I diligently make notes of the charming market towns we pass through, allowing my imagination to conjure up images of the bustling local life within.

Upon reaching Manchester Piccadilly Station, I venture forth towards the bustling bus station, eager to embark on the next leg of my adventure. The bus station buzzes with activity as buses come and go, and fellow passengers hurry about in their own quests.

Glancing at the bus timetable, I quickly locate the next bus destined for Eccles. Boarding the bus, I secure a seat near the front, granting me a prime view of the urban landscape that lies ahead. As the bus sets off,

I jotted down observations of Manchester's vibrant cityscape, complete with towering buildings and bustling streets alive with the hustle and bustle of urban life.

As we bid farewell to Manchester, the scenery gradually changes before my very eyes. Sprawling urbanity gives way to quaint residential neighbourhoods, and soon enough, we find ourselves entering Eccles. I note the landmarks and points of interest along the way, from historical buildings steeped in stories to local shops that exude an inviting charm.

Stepping off the bus, I am greeted by the warm embrace of Eccles, a town that beckons with its distinctive allure. Taking a moment to absorb the atmosphere, I make further observations of the local architecture, the variety of passers-by faces and body language, and the overall ambience that permeates Eccles.

With energy in each of my steps, I eagerly set forth to explore the wonders of Eccles. The town warmly welcomes me with its quintessentially British charm, evident from the very moment my foot graces its quaint streets. Eccles boasts well-preserved buildings that whisper tales of its past, while traditional shops and friendly locals contribute to the inviting atmosphere that envelops the town.

My adventure begins with a leisurely stroll through the town centre, allowing me to fully immerse myself in its charming architecture and soak up the vibrant ambiance. The bustling market square bustles with life, as stalls brimming with fresh produce, local crafts, and tantalising treats tantalise passers-by. Succumbing to temptation, I treat myself to an authentic Eccles cake, savouring its flaky pastry and delightful currant filling—a truly scrumptious taste of the town's culinary heritage.

Continuing on my merry way, I chance upon the iconic Eccles Town Hall, a marvel of architectural brilliance that proudly symbolises the town's civic pride. Its grand facade and intricate details speak volumes about Eccles' rich history and cultural significance. I marvel at the craftsmanship on display and admire the building's majestic presence, fully appreciating its rightful place in the make-up of the town's identity.

As I venture further into Eccles, the tranquil waters of the Bridgewater Canal beckon, serving as a testament to the town's industrial past. The canal offers a serene respite from the bustling town centre, providing picturesque views and an air of serenity. Taking a leisurely stroll along the canal towpath, I relish the peacefulness of the surroundings, admiring the graceful narrowboats gliding upon the water and immersing myself in the breathtaking beauty of nature.

Fully embracing the local atmosphere, I engage in amicable conversations with the town's residents, who warmly share their stories and offer insightful recommendations. These delightful exchanges lead me to uncover much that would have remained a mystery, including charming parks adorned with vibrant flowers, local art galleries showcasing the talents of gifted artists, and cosy tearooms that serve delectable pastries and refreshing cups of tea. Each new discovery adds another layer of delight to my experience of Eccles, deepening my appreciation for the town's unique offerings.

As the sun begins to descend, casting a warm and golden glow across the town, I find myself making my way towards 'The Ecclesian,' an apartment complex near Eccles train station. It has been an eventful experience with its fair share of ups and downs. Upon arrival, I received a warm and professional welcome from the staff, who efficiently checked me in. The lobby exuded a modern and sophisticated charm, setting the stage for a luxurious stay.

Stepping into my apartment, I was initially impressed by the elegant design and contemporary furnishings. However, I quickly discovered that the bed was disappointingly soft, causing me to sink uncomfortably when I laid on it. Despite this setback, the apartment maintained a tranquil ambiance and featured tasteful decor, creating a pleasant overall atmosphere.

When it came to dining at the on-site restaurant, I encountered some disappointment. The food failed to meet my expectations in terms of freshness, and the portion sizes left much to be desired. It was a letdown considering The Ecclesian's reputation and cost.

Nonetheless, I took a moment to appreciate the overall ambiance and attention to detail of the apartment. While the comfort of the bed was lacking, the rest of the space exuded tranquillity and sophistication, allowing for relaxation and reflection.

In conclusion, my stay at The Ecclesian had its ups and downs. The upscale atmosphere, accompanied by the attentive service and convenient location, were commendable aspects of my experience. However, the disappointing comfort of the bed and the underwhelming dining experience were notable drawbacks.

Reflecting on my time spent in Eccles, a wave of opportunities presented themselves to wholeheartedly immerse myself in the town's authentic British charm. From the friendly encounters with locals to the captivating sights that unfolded at every turn, Eccles has left an indelible mark on my adventurous journey. As I drift off into a peaceful slumber, I eagerly anticipate the dawning of a new day, knowing that it will bring with it a fresh array of treasures and experiences, further enriching my alphabetical tour through England."

Eccles

ECCLES TO FARNBOROUGH

It was time to bid a fond farewell to the delightful town of Eccles and embark on the next leg of my whimsical adventure towards the captivating destination of Farnborough. An early start was required, and most of the morning would be spent in transit. Little did I know that this chapter of my journey would be filled to the brim with unexpected surprises and heartwarming conversations, adding a delightful account of experiences to my exploration.

As I prepared myself for the voyage from Eccles to Farnborough, a tingling anticipation danced through my veins. With an intrepid spirit as my guide, I eagerly set forth on this beguiling narrative, eager to chronicle each captivating moment that lay ahead.

Beginning my expedition at Eccles, I made my way to the local train station, alive with a vibrant flurry of activity. Commuters hurried about; their eagerness palpable as they rushed towards their intended destinations. Acquiring my ticket with a flourish, I boarded the train bound for Farnborough, seeking out a cosy nook by the window, where I could revel in the unfolding adventure.

Stepping onto the train at Eccles Station, I couldn't help but notice the lively atmosphere buzzing around me. People from all walks of life bustled about, each with their own destination in mind. I adjusted my smartly dressed attire, ready to take on the role of a ticket inspector for the day.

The train ride from Eccles to Manchester Piccadilly was a short one, a mere 15 minutes whisking through the picturesque countryside. I made my way through the carriages and found my seat.

Upon reaching Manchester Piccadilly, my fellow passengers and I bid each other farewell, their eyes lingering on my smartly dressed figure. It was a rewarding feeling, knowing that I had played a small part in making their journey a more enjoyable one.

From there, we embarked on the next leg of the adventure, boarding a train bound for London Euston Station. The hours slipped away as the train smoothly glided through the changing landscapes, eventually bringing us to the bustling heart of the capital city.

Following my instructions, we ventured into the depths of the London Underground, finding ourselves on the southbound Victoria Line platform at Vauxhall Station. The efficiency of the underground system was truly remarkable, whisking us away to our next destination with ease.

With our spirits high and anticipation building, we transferred to a train heading towards Farnborough at Vauxhall Station. The journey was a delightful one, offering glimpses of the lush English countryside as I chatted with a passenger and shared stories of our histories and travels.

Finally, the train announced our arrival at Farnborough Station. We gathered our belongings and bid farewell to each other; the memories of our shared journey forever etched in our minds.

I almost fell off the train at Farnborough Station, but once recomposed, I found myself enveloped in the captivating bustle of this vibrant town. The air buzzed with a delightful blend of activity and suburban charm, inviting me to revel in the delightful sights and sounds that unfolded before me.

During my meandering exploration, I had the good fortune of engaging in captivating conversations with the locals. They regaled me with tales of Farnborough's rich history, passionately sharing its profound connection to the aviation industry and its role as a dynamic hub of innovation. Their fervent enthusiasm ignited a renewed appreciation within me for Farnborough's significance, infusing my journey with a sense of awe.

Amidst my wanderings, a chance encounter with a homeless gentleman seeking solace on a weathered bench captivated my attention. Intrigued by his presence, I approached him with a warm smile and engaged in a heartfelt conversation. In the exchange of words, he painted vivid brushstrokes of his life, sharing tales of resilience, struggles, and dreams that lingered within his soul. His unwavering spirit and kindness left an indelible impression, serving as a poignant reminder of the transformative power of empathy and understanding.

In the evening, after a fulfilling day of exploring and enjoying the confines of Farnborough, I returned with a bag of fresh groceries, eager to prepare a delightful dinner in the well-equipped kitchen. I decided to go for a classic British favourite and whipped up a scrumptious fish and chips meal. I prepared crispy battered cod fillets, frying them until golden and succulent. Alongside the fish, I sliced up some fluffy potatoes and fried them to perfection, creating the quintessential chips. I sprinkled a touch of salt over the chips, giving them that irresistible flavour. To complete the dish, I served it with a dollop of tartare sauce and a side of mushy peas, adding that authentic touch. As I took the first bite, the crunch of the batter and the tender fish melted in my mouth, instantly transporting me to a traditional British fish and chip shop. It was a truly satisfying evening, relishing the taste of my homemade fish and chips while enjoying the cosy ambiance of the flat.

However, the night brought with it a whimsical dance of restlessness, as the unfamiliar noises and the adjustment to a new environment tugged at the edges of sleep. However, as the morning sun shyly peeked over the horizon, I arose, groggily yet determined, ready to continue my merry expedition through the breathtaking landscapes of England. With a touch of weariness and a heart brimming with anticipation, I cast my thoughts toward the enchanting city of Gloucester, eagerly awaiting the treasures it held and the whimsical memories yet to be woven into the fabric of my journey. Little did I know what grand adventures awaited, but with an ardent sparkle in my eye and a buoyant spring in my step, I embraced them wholeheartedly, eager to discover the wonders that lay just beyond the horizon.

haart
haart

FARNBOROUGH TO GLOUCESTER

In the little-known town of Farnborough, a place that had yet to make its mark on the map of whimsical wonders, I found myself preparing to bid it farewell. With a cup of tea in hand and a towel conveniently tucked under my arm (one must always be prepared for the unexpected, you see), I embarked on the next leg of my journey. Gloucester, a city steeped in history and intrigue, awaited my arrival, its secrets whispering on the breeze.

Now in the process of leaving Farnborough behind, I made my way to the bustling railway station, a hive of activity that could rival the most frenetic of marketplaces. The ticket in my pocket felt like a passport to another realm, as I joined the throng of eager travellers all with a destination in mind. The station attendant, ever the bearer of knowledge and directions, bestowed upon me a ticket to Gloucester with a cheerful smile and a gentle reminder to mind the gap. Allow me to add an account of getting lost trying to find the station, but having plenty of time to spare finding it with the help of a shop assistant.

As I navigated my way through the labyrinthine streets of Farnborough, my excitement grew with each stride. The sun cast its warm glow upon the bustling town, and the air hummed with the energy of people going about their daily lives. Finally, after a few wrong turns and detours, I spotted the familiar signposts leading me to the railway station.

The station stood tall and proud, its architecture blending the charm of yesteryear with the modernity of the present. The sound of trains arriving and departing reverberated through the air, creating a symphony of motion and anticipation. It was as if the station itself was alive, pulsating with the tales of countless journeys taken and dreams fulfilled.

I joined the throng of fellow travellers, their faces adorned with expressions of wanderlust and adventure. The ticket in my pocket felt like a magical token, granting me access to distant lands and uncharted horizons. With a quick step and an eye to the shortest queue, I eagerly made my way to arrays of ticket counters, where various station attendants awaited.

The attendant, a cheerful individual with a cap perched atop their head, greeted me with a warm smile. They possessed a wealth of knowledge, well-versed in the art of guiding lost souls like myself. As I approached, they kindly asked, "Where are you headed, sir?"

"Gloucester," I replied, my voice brimming with enthusiasm.

The attendant nodded and swiftly retrieved a ticket from a well-organised drawer. With a gentle flick of their wrist, they handed it to me, along with a cheerful reminder to "mind the gap." Grateful for their assistance, I thanked them and proceeded towards the platform.

While the minutes ticked away, I realised that I had some spare time on my hands. Eager to explore a little more before embarking on my train ride, I ventured outside the station and found myself amidst a bustling high street. The shops lined the avenue, displaying their wares. I entered a nearby boutique, where a friendly shop assistant greeted me. Explaining my predicament of trying to find the station, she graciously offered her assistance. Armed with their guidance, I retraced my steps and soon found myself back at the bustling hive of the railway station.

Returning to the platform, I caught sight of my approaching train in the distance. The rhythmic chugging and the melodic whistle filled the air, heralding its imminent arrival. Excitement surged within me as I boarded the train, my ticket guiding me towards new experiences and the enchanting destination of Gloucester.

Leaving Farnborough behind, I settled into my seat, eagerly anticipating the sights, sounds, and discoveries that awaited me on this exhilarating journey.

Stepping aboard the train, I found a window seat, my loyal vantage point for witnessing the wonders that lay beyond the smudged glass. As the train jolted to life, the rhythmic rub of wheel turns on tracks became a plethora of movement, the soundtrack to my odyssey. We glided through the countryside, passing fields of grazing cows and rolling hills that seemed to sway in time with the train's rhythm.

But alas, as is often the case in the grandeur of existence, our journey was not without its unexpected detours. At Reading Station, chaos erupted like a flock of indignant seagulls with their chips stolen. A fellow traveller, imbued with a potent combination of merriment and spirits, became the centre of attention, commanding a stage that was both bewildering and hilarious. The station staff, valiant heroes of order and sanity, rallied to tame the tempestuous scene, calling upon the authorities with a flick of their wrists.

In the midst of this lively interlude, a peculiar camaraderie blossomed among the passengers. We exchanged bemused glances and chuckled together, finding solace in the shared absurdity of the situation. The delay, far from dampening our spirits, became a catalyst for fleeting connections and laughter-laden tales.

With the arrival of the local constabulary, adorned in their resplendent uniforms, the scene began to simmer down like a pot of tea left to steep. Their authoritative yet compassionate demeanour restored a sense of order, gently guiding the spirited soul away from the platform and towards a more suitable stage for their performance.

As the clock ticked and the situation resolved, we were guided back onto the train, ready to resume our journey to Gloucester. With the lingering laughter and newfound camaraderie, we embarked once more, our spirits undeterred by the whims of fate.

The train glided through the changing landscape, teasing glimpses of the wonders that awaited us. Ancient villages materialised like apparitions, their thatched roofs and cobbled streets a charming testament to the passage of time. The majestic River Severn accompanied us, its waters shimmering under the gentle caress of sunlight, as if whispering secrets only the wind could comprehend.

At last, Gloucester Station emerged from the horizon, its grandeur a beacon of history and intrigue. Stepping onto the platform, I found myself immersed in a city that embraced both the echoes of the past and the vibrant pulse of the present. Gloucester Cathedral, a marvel of Gothic architecture, reached for the heavens, its spires piercing the sky like a curious alien species attempting communication.

Wandering through the city's labyrinthine streets, I discovered hidden gems at every turn. The Gloucester Docks, once a bustling centre of maritime activity, now stood as a testament to adaptation and reinvention. Narrowboats bobbed gently in the water, their colourful facades reflecting in the ripples, as if painted by a cosmic artist. The aroma of culinary delights wafted through the air, mingling with the laughter and conversations that filled the dockside eateries, a tempting array of tastes and stories.

As twilight settled over the city, I sought refuge in a cosy hotel, its walls whispering tales of travellers past. The bed welcomed me like a long-lost friend, cradling me in its embrace as dreams wove peculiar images and half-remembered fragments.

However, hunger still lingered after my eye-opening day. It was too late to dine at a restaurant, besides which, weariness was tugged at my bones, urging me to rest. In an unusual departure from my usual routine, I decided to order a pizza takeaway. It seemed like the perfect solution, allowing me to satiate my hunger without venturing out into the night.

The aroma of freshly baked pizza wafted through the air as I eagerly unwrapped the steaming box. It was a comforting sight—a medley of colourful toppings artfully arranged on a bed of golden crust. Each slice held the promise of savoury delight, and I savoured every bite in the cosy embrace of my hotel room. It was a departure from the usual dining experience, but it brought a sense of comfort and convenience in that moment of weariness.

As I settled into the soft embrace of the bed, my mind drifting between the fragments of dreams and the taste of pizza on my tongue, I couldn't help but appreciate the simplicity of the moment. Sometimes, even the most unexpected choices can bring a touch of comfort and nourishment, allowing weary travellers like myself to find solace in the simplest pleasures.

Gloucester had woven its enchantment around me, leaving an indelible mark on my journey. The city's history and vibrant spirit had seeped into my very being, igniting a curiosity that could not be extinguished. As I drifted into sleep, my mind filled with visions of the adventures that lay ahead, I knew that Gloucester was merely the beginning—a prelude to the wonders that awaited me in the vast expanse of the plains.

As the sun peered over the horizon, casting a golden hue across the land, I found myself embarking on yet another curious expedition. The peculiar town of Gloucester had bid me farewell, and my whimsical journey led me to the realm of Harrogate. With a towel securely fastened to my rucksack (for one must always be prepared for the unexpected, especially when travelling through the density of England), I set forth, traversing the vast network of transport.

The day promised a medley of trains, buses, and who knows what other fantastical contraptions would cross my path. With each transfer, I dived headfirst into a dance of interchanges, a choreography of schedules and platforms that tested the limits of my temporal fortitude. But fear not, for I was armed with a pocketful of whimsy and a resolve as strong as titanium dental floss.

Navigating the labyrinthine depths of Birmingham New Street Station, I became a speck in the grand picture of hurried commuters and bewildered travellers. The station, a behemoth of steel and glass, towered above me, its platforms stretching out like tentacles of an interstellar cephalopod. Amongst the bewildering signs and the cacophony of announcements, I momentarily lost my way, as if caught in the gravitational pull of a cosmic joke.

With a dash of intuition and a sprinkle of good fortune, I found myself on the right platform, poised to board the train to Harrogate. The carriages stood before me; an assortment of metal boxes ready to transport me to a realm shrouded in intrigue. As I settled into my seat, an unexpected visitor appeared—an extraterrestrial ticket inspector, with a peculiar complexion and an uncanny ability to recite train regulations in binary code.

To my astonishment, the inspector informed me that the seat I had chosen was, in fact, not mine. With a flurry of apologies and the occasional sigh of resignation, I vacated the seat, destined to spend the remainder of the journey perched atop a luggage rack like a wayward gnome. Oh, the trials and tribulations of interstellar travel!

Despite the seat shuffle and the occasional turbulence encountered, I eventually arrived at Harrogate Station. Stepping onto the platform, I was greeted by a town that teetered on the precipice of peculiarity. Harrogate, a place where the ordinary and the extraordinary danced a tango of perplexity, beckoned me with open arms.

As I ventured into the heart of this enigmatic town, I stumbled upon hidden gems tucked between the mundane facades. Quaint cafes appeared like mirages in the desert of normalcy, serving elixirs of caffeinated wisdom and pastries infused with the essence of whimsy. The streets, lined with buildings that seemed to defy the laws of architectural logic, whispered tales of eccentric residents and secret societies hidden behind inconspicuous doors.

In Harrogate, time itself seemed to fold and twist, playing tricks on unsuspecting wanderers. I found myself in a maze of narrow alleys and hidden courtyards, where every corner revealed a new twist in the narrative of this peculiar place. The voices of long-forgotten poets echoed through the air, as if the very atmosphere were imbued with the ink of their words.

At the heart of Harrogate, the grandeur of the Royal Pump Room Museum stood as a testament to the town's storied past. Its hallowed halls housed a treasure trove of art and artefacts, each whispering tales of bygone eras and enigmatic creators. I meandered through the rooms, my eyes tracing the brushstrokes of masterpieces and my imagination filling in the gaps of history.

With the day drawing to a close, I sought refuge in a quintessential British inn, its thatched roof and timbered walls exuding an air of rustic charm. The innkeeper, a jolly soul with a twinkle in his eye, regaled me with stories of local legends and the mischievous spirits that haunted the ancient corridors. As I settled into a cosy room adorned with floral wallpaper, I drifted into a slumber, the dreams of Harrogate swirling through my mind.

The following morning, fortified by a traditional full English breakfast and a pot of steaming tea, I bid farewell to the inn and the delightful inhabitants of Harrogate. With a rucksack laden with memories and a heart filled with gratitude, I embarked on the next leg of my whimsical adventure. For the cosmos is vast and teeming with wonders, waiting to be discovered by those willing to embrace the peculiarities of the journey. And so, I set forth, ready to embrace the unknown and dance through the English scenery once more.

HARROGATE TO IPSWICH

As I embarked on the train from Harrogate to Leeds, I was filled with anticipation for the brisk 30-minute journey that lay ahead. The train carriages were bustling with individuals immersed in their daily affairs, and I managed to secure a seat to relish the passage.

Upon reaching Leeds Station, I navigated through the throng, searching for the platform of my subsequent train to Ipswich. It was then that I noticed a fatigued mother grappling with a wailing infant. The poor child seemed exhausted, and I empathised with the mother's predicament.

Having settled into my seat on the train bound for Peterborough, I found myself a few rows behind the distressed mother and her vocal offspring. Goodness gracious, the infant's cries reverberated throughout the carriage, making it challenging for everyone to concentrate.

Despite the tumult, the mother handled the situation admirably, making earnest attempts to soothe her little one. The passengers, in turn, expressed their solidarity with sympathetic glances and friendly smiles.

The journey from Leeds to Peterborough meandered through picturesque countryside, offering glimpses of captivating landscapes. I tried to appreciate the scenery, but the incessant wailing made it a bit of a struggle.

Nevertheless, the mother exhibited commendable patience, garnering admiration from all on board for her efforts. When we eventually arrived at Peterborough Station, there was a collective sigh of relief. I wished the mother tranquillity on the next leg of her journey to London

King's Cross Station, hoping for a change of scene to bring solace to both her and the baby.

Having enjoyed a brief respite at London King's Cross Station, I eagerly embarked on the subsequent phase of my journey – the excursion from King's Cross to Ipswich. The platform buzzed with activity as fellow passengers hurriedly made their way to their respective trains, their conversations blending with the announcements resonating throughout the station.

Identifying the correct platform, I swiftly boarded the train bound for Ipswich. As the train departed, I settled into my seat, gazing out of the window to witness the gradual transition from the urban sprawl of London to the serene English countryside.

The train journey from King's Cross to Ipswich was a harmonious blend of tranquillity and anticipation. The rhythmic swaying of the carriage provided a soothing backdrop, lulling me into a contemplative state. The passing scenery painted a picturesque tableau of rolling hills, meandering rivers, and quaint villages.

Throughout the journey, the train made several stops, affording me glimpses into the lives of fellow passengers who embarked or disembarked at these stations. I observed fellow travellers engrossed in literature, engaging in lively conversations, or simply lost in introspection. Each stop injected fresh energy into the voyage: a weaving of human connections.

As Ipswich drew nearer, the landscape underwent a captivating transformation, fusing coastal splendour with architectural charm. The train gracefully traversed verdant fields, while the gentle sea breeze teased my senses, signifying the proximity of the coastline.

Upon arrival at Ipswich Station, a profound sense of achievement washed over me. The journey from King's Cross had unfolded seamlessly, offering a delightful glimpse into the diverse fabric of the English countryside.

Stepping out of Ipswich Station, I immediately felt the pulse of the town's rich history and maritime heritage. The proximity to the river Orwell added a distinct charm, and I eagerly made my way towards the town centre, ready to unravel the mysteries that awaited me. The towering Ipswich Town Hall stood as a grand symbol of the town's past, beckoning me to delve deeper into its fascinating heritage.

Wandering through the streets of Ipswich, I found myself immersed in an accolade of architectural wonders. The Ancient House, with its intricately carved timber frames, stood as a testament to the craftsmanship of a bygone era. As I marvelled at its beauty, I couldn't help but imagine the stories that echoed within its walls. And then, there was the magnificent Christchurch Mansion, a stately presence that commanded attention and left me in awe of its grandeur. Every corner seemed to hold a piece of history, inviting me to discover the narratives woven into Ipswich's past.

Continuing my journey, I found myself drawn to the vibrant waterfront. The Ipswich Waterfront Marina bustled with life as yachts and sailboats bobbed gently on the river's surface. I settled into a riverside cafe, basking in the warm sunlight, and indulged in a leisurely lunch. The sight of boats gliding by and the rhythmic clapping of the water created a tranquil ambiance that rejuvenated my spirit, providing a moment of calm amidst the buzz of the town.

After satisfying my appetite, I ventured deeper into Ipswich's cultural realm. The Ipswich Museum, housed within a magnificent Victorian building, captivated me with its vast collection of artifacts. From ancient relics to natural wonders, the museum offered a glimpse into the region's rich heritage and ignited my imagination. It was like embarking on a time-traveling adventure, where each exhibit told a unique story and transported me to different eras.

At the Ipswich Art Gallery, I found myself surrounded by captivating contemporary artworks that pushed the boundaries of creativity. Each piece spoke a language of its own, evoking emotions and provoking thought. I immersed myself in the vibrant colours, intricate details, and thought-provoking concepts, discovering new perspectives and expanding my appreciation for artistic expression.

During my exploration, fortune smiled upon me as I stumbled upon a small gallery tucked away in a hidden corner of Ipswich. Inside, a local artist proudly showcased their works, each canvas telling a personal story and reflecting the artist's unique vision. Engaging in conversation, the artist shared their passion for Ipswich's artistic community and revealed the existence of hidden art studios scattered throughout the town. Intrigued by this insider knowledge, I made a mental note to seek out these hidden gems, eager to witness the creativity that thrived within Ipswich's artistic soul.

I stayed at the 2-star hotel called the 'Great White Horse' in Ipswich, immersing myself in its historic ambiance. The friendly staff warmly welcomed me, setting the tone for a memorable experience. My room, though modest, provided a comfortable retreat from the bustling world outside.

In the evening, I decided to dine at the hotel's restaurant, hoping to savour a delightful culinary experience. The meal turned out to be satisfactory, although it left a dent in my wallet, as fine dining often does. The menu boasted an array of dishes, each with its own unique flair. I opted for a succulent grilled steak accompanied by a medley of roasted vegetables, perfectly cooked to bring out their natural flavours. The presentation was aesthetically pleasing, showcasing the chef's attention to detail. While the meal didn't exceed my expectations, it provided a satisfying dining experience within the convenience of the hotel.

After dinner, I sought relaxation at the hotel's bar, enjoying a soothing ambiance and the company of another fellow traveller. Engaging in light conversation and laughter, I savoured a well-crafted cocktail that served as the perfect nightcap. As fatigue gradually overtook me, I retired to my room and surrendered myself to the embrace of a remarkably comfortable bed. Its soft sheets and plump pillows cradled me in a cocoon of tranquillity, ensuring a restful night's sleep that recharged my weary body.

However, the next morning posed a challenge—I had an early start to catch a train to Newcastle, with a departure time set for the unforgiving hour of 05:10. Regrettably, there would be no time to indulge in a leisurely breakfast. Instead, I would have to rely on the anticipation of a warm cup of coffee and a quick snack to fuel my journey.

As I bid farewell to the 'Great White Horse' and the memorable experiences it offered, I couldn't help but appreciate the quaint charm of the hotel, the modest yet comfortable room, and the mixed feelings I had about the expensive yet satisfactory meal. It was a fleeting encounter, but one that left an indelible impression, reminding me that even in the realm of two-star accommodations, memorable moments and unique experiences await those who seek them.

IPSWICH TO JARROW

It was a 4:30 am wake-up call as I I roused myself from slumber, compelled by the anticipation of an imminent adventure. Swiftly navigating the hushed corridors of Ipswich Station, I boarded the train destined for Newcastle, my enthusiasm bubbling over. Seated comfortably, I envisaged the delightful revelations and concealed gems awaiting discovery during this extensive sojourn—an expedition poised to be my lengthiest rail expedition, spanning a duration of approximately four and a half hours to reach Newcastle, with another leg to Jarrow.

The train commenced its journey, bidding farewell to the bustling urbanity of Ipswich. Gazing through the window, I witnessed a metamorphosis in the scenery. The charming panorama of East Anglian countryside unfolded before my eyes, with undulating hills, expansive fields, and picturesque hamlets.

The golden wheat fields swayed in rhythmic unison, a mesmerising spectacle enhanced by a gentle breeze. It seemed as though nature had cast a magical aura upon each stalk of wheat, transforming the landscape into a glistening sea of gold. In my imagination, I frolicked through the fields, arms outstretched, feeling the caress of wheat against my fingertips.

Quaint villages adorned the countryside, their thatched-roof cottages exuding an ageless allure. Vibrant flower gardens bloomed, injecting joyous hues into the idyllic scenes. I envisioned knocking on the doors of these cottages, welcomed by locals offering freshly baked scones and steaming pots of tea—an embodiment of rural England's warmth and hospitality.

Advancing northward, the train traversed the counties of Suffolk and Norfolk, unveiling a whimsical ambiance reminiscent of a storybook setting. Enchanting woods and forests emerged, their trees reaching skywards like ancient sentinels. I half-expected to glimpse fairies flitting among the branches or woodland creatures peeking mischievously from behind the trunks.

The journey extended into Durham, a city I had recently explored, where the scenery assumed a regal allure. Verdant hills enveloped in lush greenery conveyed a sense of serenity and natural beauty. I envisioned myself frolicking through meadows, collecting wildflowers and relishing the invigorating air.

After a brief 30-minute interlude, I changed trains at Newcastle, poised to continue the odyssey to Jarrow. The subsequent leg of the journey meandered through picturesque countryside, adorned with rolling hills, quaint villages, and meandering rivers. Lush greenery and a tranquil ambiance painted a serene backdrop for the majority of the expedition. Approaching Jarrow, anticipation surged, eager to explore a town steeped in historical resonance.

As Jarrow drew near, the town's industrial legacy unfolded. Dockyards and industrial edifices bore witness to a bygone era of history and industrious toil. Imaginations stirred as I envisioned the town in its zenith, shipbuilders bustling about, constructing majestic vessels destined for the high seas. The echoes of Jarrow's maritime past resonated in the air, beckoning a deeper exploration into its rich history.

Disembarking at Jarrow Station, I found myself immediately captivated by the town's distinctive character. The imposing Jarrow Hall, a Georgian mansion and Anglo-Saxon farm, stood as an emblem of the town's ancient history. Its grandeur inspired contemplation of the generations that had resided within its walls.

Keen to immerse myself in Jarrow's history, I ventured towards the venerable Jarrow Monastery, also known as St. Paul's Church. Crossing its ancient threshold, I felt transported through time. The weathered stone arches and interiors bore testimony to the spiritual devotion that once filled this sacred space. Almost audible were the whispered prayers and chants of long-gone monks, their spectral presence lingering in the air.

Having delved into the historical treasures of the town, I embarked on a leisurely riverside stroll along the banks of the River Tyne. The tranquil waters mirrored the town's calm and peaceful nature, while the iconic Tyne Bridge and the modern architecture of the Gateshead Millennium Bridge imparted a touch of contemporary charm. It was a delightful juxtaposition of the old and the new, a testament to the harmonious coexistence of history and progress.

My perambulations led me to a bustling market, where vibrant stalls beckoned with an array of goods. Engulfed in a lively cacophony of colours, scents, and sounds, I savoured the taste of locally produced delights, admired handmade crafts, and engaged in animated conversations with passionate vendors. The market served as a microcosm of Jarrow's community spirit, a realm where stories were shared, the trials of daily life bemoaned, and laughter resonated on other occasions.

With hunger assuaged, I pursued the alluring aroma of traditional North East cuisine to a welcoming local pub. The warm ambience enveloped me as I settled into a cosy seat, perusing a menu that showcased culinary masterpieces celebrating the region's gastronomic heritage. I indulged in a hearty repast, relishing each mouthful and complementing it with a pint of locally brewed ale. The flavours danced on my palate, a delectable flavours paying homage to the region's rich culinary traditions, even if they weren't particularly conducive to one's well-being.

My night's lodging was a capacious ground-floor flat in a stately period terrace. Tastefully adorned with relatively new fittings, it did contend with a minor damp issue, abated by the presence of air purifiers. Nestled in a tranquil cul-de-sac near the Metro and adjacent to a park, its location proved exceptionally convenient for morning transit.

As the night sky adorned itself with a velvety expanse of stars, I nestled into the soft sheets of my bed, sporting a contented smile. My dreams wove themselves with the enchantment of Jarrow, a tribute to the extraordinary places and people that render England an exceptional destination.

Awakening with the first rays of dawn peeking through the curtains, I greeted the new day with a rekindled excitement. The escapades in Jarrow had ignited a fervour of curiosity and wanderlust within me, burning more brightly than ever. Bidding Jarrow a swift adieu, I eagerly embarked towards the historic town of Kendal, prepared to uncover its own treasures and weave fresh memories into the network of my travels.

JARROW TO KENDAL

I found myself at Jarrow Station, where the platform hummed with the comings and goings of busy commuters. Standing amidst the crowd, I noticed the familiar blue and yellow Metro train pulling up, ready to whisk me away on the first leg of my journey. I got onboard and settled into a comfortable seat near the window. As the train departed with a gentle jolt, I observed the countryside passing by— fields, charming villages, and lush green pastures. Lost in my thoughts, time slipped away as I marvelled at the beauty of North East England.

Soon enough, the train slowed down, and I caught sight of the recognisable landmarks of Newcastle upon Tyne. We arrived at the bustling Newcastle upon Tyne Station, and I gathered my belongings, preparing to continue my journey. Stepping onto the platform, I followed the signs to the mainline trains. It didn't take long for me to locate the train heading towards Carlisle. With a sense of anticipation, I boarded the train and settled into a comfortable seat. Leaving Newcastle upon Tyne behind, the train rippling along, traversing picturesque landscapes and charming towns.

The journey to Carlisle lasted approximately 2 hours, but I didn't mind the passing of time. I immersed myself in a good book, occasionally stealing glances out of the window to admire the breathtaking countryside rolling by. The train journey provided a peaceful interlude, allowing me to unwind and savour the journey at my own pace.

Finally, the train announced our arrival in Carlisle. Stepping off the train, I took a moment to stretch my legs and inhale the crisp air. Carlisle Station buzzed with activity, bustling with travellers from various destinations.

To reach my final destination of Kendal, I made my way to the platform for the next train. Fortunately, the wait was brief, and soon I found myself aboard a train bound for Kendal. The journey from Carlisle to Kendal was relatively short, lasting around 20 to 30 minutes.

As we approached Kendal, a wave of excitement washed over me. The train gradually decelerated, and I eagerly peered out of the window, eager to explore this picturesque town nestled in the heart of the Lake District. With a final gentle halt, the train came to a stop at Kendal Station.

I alighted from the train, filled with a sense of accomplishment and wonder. My journey from Jarrow to Newcastle upon Tyne, then Carlisle, and finally Kendal had been a delightful adventure, showcasing the beauty of the region's landscapes and connecting me with vibrant cities and charming towns along the way.

Cobblestone streets meandered through the town centre, lined with quaint shops and inviting cafes. The scent of freshly baked goods wafted through the air, tempting me to indulge in the local culinary delights.

One of the highlights of my visit was the enchanting Kendal Castle, perched on a hilltop overlooking the town. Ascending the worn steps, I felt a sense of awe at the castle's weathered grandeur. From the highest point, I beheld a breathtaking panorama of the surrounding countryside, a patchwork of fields and forests that stretched towards the horizon. It was as if I had stumbled upon a hidden realm, a place frozen in time, where stories of knights and fair maidens still whispered on the breeze.

Exploring Kendal's winding streets, I uncovered hidden treasures at every corner. Charming tea rooms enticed me with their delicate china and freshly brewed pots of tea, while independent boutiques offered unique souvenirs and handmade crafts. I couldn't resist the allure of Kendal Mint Cake, a local specialty that provided a sweet burst of energy as I continued my explorations.

To delve deeper into the town's history, I visited the Kendal Museum, a treasure trove of artifacts and exhibits that shed light on the region's past. From Roman relics to displays showcasing the town's industrial heritage, the museum painted a vivid picture of Kendal's rich tapestry of stories. I immersed myself in the tales of bygone eras, feeling a deep sense of connection to the town and its inhabitants throughout the ages.

In Kendal, as twilight settled, I sought refuge in a charming inn nestled among the town's historic buildings. The cosy room offered respite after a day filled with adventure, its soft bed beckoning me to unwind and recharge. But not before savouring a delicious meal at a local restaurant, where I had the pleasure of encountering a waiter who resembled the iconic character Manuel from the beloved sitcom "Fawlty Towers."

Inside the restaurant, the waiter's endearing clumsiness and enthusiastic manner added a touch of comedy to the evening, evoking fond memories of the classic comedy series. Amidst laughter and playful banter, I relished the regional flavours on my plate, enjoying a delectable dish of succulent roast lamb, accompanied by a medley of seasonal vegetables. The tender meat melted in my mouth, while the perfectly cooked vegetables provided a delightful balance of textures and tastes.

As the atmosphere buzzed with animated conversations and clinking glasses, I couldn't help but appreciate the conviviality of the moment. The restaurant exuded warmth and charm, fostering a sense of camaraderie among the diners. Toasting to the joys of exploration and the pleasures of good company, I savoured each bite, fully immersing myself in the culinary experience.

Leaving the restaurant with a satisfied palate and a heart filled with laughter, I made my way back to the comforting embrace of the inn. The memory of that memorable dining experience lingered in my mind, a testament to the magic that can be found in unexpected encounters and the simple pleasures of life.

With a contented heart and a mind brimming with memories, I slipped into a peaceful slumber, ready to embrace the next leg of my A-to-Z journey. Kendal had cast its spell upon me, leaving an indelible mark on my soul. I couldn't wait to continue my odyssey, ready to uncover the wonders that awaited me in the enchanting town of Lichfield, eagerly anticipating the tales I would weave and the experiences I would cherish along the way.

KENDAL TO LICHFIELD

As the sun rose over Kendal, casting a warm golden glow on the town, I bid farewell to its picturesque streets and set off on the next leg of my extraordinary A-to-Z journey towards Lichfield. Excitement filled the air as I boarded the train, eager to uncover the hidden gems and delightful surprises that awaited me in this vibrant town.

Leaving behind the tranquil beauty of Kendal, the train traversed through the captivating landscapes of northern England. Rolling hills and lush green fields stretched as far as the eye could see, dotted with grazing sheep and quaint farmhouses. It was a scene straight out of a postcard, with each passing mile revealing a new vista more awe-inspiring than the last.

As we journeyed southward, the train meandered through charming villages and historic market towns that appeared frozen in time. Quaint cottages with thatched roofs lined the streets, their colourful gardens blooming with vibrant flowers. I couldn't help but imagine the stories that reverberated within the walls of these timeless abodes, tales of generations past and the simple joys of rural life.

However, amidst the serene scenery, an unexpected incident briefly disrupted the peaceful atmosphere. A fellow passenger suddenly fell ill, prompting a wave of concern among those nearby. In a moment of panic, he pulled the emergency cord, bringing the train to an immediate halt. The piercing sound of the alarm reverberated through the carriages, momentarily jolting us from our reverie.

As the train came to a stop, the conductor swiftly assessed the situation, ensuring that the passenger received the necessary care. After a brief but anxious delay of approximately 20 minutes, it became apparent that the individual's condition had stabilised, much to everyone's relief. A palpable sense of shared concern hung in the air, fostering a temporary camaraderie among the passengers who had witnessed the unforeseen turn of events.

Curiosity piqued within me, as I had often wondered what would transpire in the event of an emergency cord being pulled. This unexpected occurrence provided me with an unintended glimpse into the protocol and response mechanisms employed by the railway staff, ensuring the well-being and safety of passengers on board.

As the journey resumed, the train gradually regained its rhythmic motion, soothing us with the familiar hum of the tracks. The incident, though fleeting, served as a reminder of the unpredictable nature of life's voyage and the significance of compassion and solidarity during times of uncertainty. And as we continued on our southward path, the enchanting countryside once again enveloped us, captivating our hearts with its timeless allure and sparking our imaginations with its whispered tales.

Passing through Staffordshire, the landscape transformed into a patchwork of fields and hedgerows, where rabbits darted playfully and birds soared overhead. The gentle hills rolled on, revealing hidden valleys and picturesque woodlands, inviting me to explore their secrets. The train's rhythmic metallic concords seemed to harmonise with the natural rhythm of the countryside, creating a soothing movement and tranquillity.

Approaching Lichfield, the train offered tantalising glimpses of the town's architectural treasures. Lichfield Cathedral, with its majestic spires reaching towards the heavens, commanded attention and admiration. Its intricate stonework and awe-inspiring presence hinted at a rich history that waited to be discovered. I eagerly awaited the moment when I could step off the train and immerse myself in the captivating stories of Lichfield's past and present.

As the train pulled into Lichfield Station, I disembarked with a sense of anticipation. The town greeted me with open arms, its streets bustling with energy and a vibrant atmosphere. I set off on foot, ready to explore the enchanting corners and hidden nooks that Lichfield had to offer.

Walking through the town's historic centre, I marvelled at the architectural wonders that surrounded me. Georgian and Tudor-style buildings stood proudly, their intricate details showcasing the craftsmanship of bygone eras. Quaint alleyways and cobbled streets led me on a whimsical journey, each turn revealing a new delightful surprise.

One of the highlights of my visit was a visit to Lichfield Cathedral, an architectural marvel that left me in awe. Stepping through its grand doors, I found myself transported into a world of serenity and spirituality. The soft glow of stained-glass windows bathed the interior in a kaleidoscope of colours, while the soaring arches and intricate carvings whispered tales of devotion and artistry. Climbing to the top of the tower, I was rewarded with breathtaking panoramic views of the town and its picturesque surroundings, a sight that will forever be etched in my memory.

Exploring Lichfield's vibrant market, I was greeted by a cascade of sights, sounds, and aromas. Stalls brimmed with an abundance of fresh produce, locally crafted goods, and mouth-watering delicacies. I couldn't resist sampling the delectable treats on offer, from artisanal cheeses to freshly baked pastries. The lively atmosphere and friendly banter of the market vendors added an extra layer of charm to the experience, making me feel like a welcomed guest in this bustling community.

To delve deeper into Lichfield's rich heritage, I visited the Samuel Johnson Birthplace Museum. Stepping into the restored 18th-century townhouse, I embarked on a journey through the life and works of the renowned lexicographer. Johnson's personal belongings, including his handwritten manuscripts and beloved books, offered a fascinating glimpse into the mind of a literary genius. As I wandered through the rooms where Johnson once lived and worked, I felt a profound connection to the man who shaped the English language and left an indelible mark on the literary world.

As the day turned into evening, I found myself in need of a well-deserved rest. Lichfield's hospitality industry did not disappoint, as I settled into a charming bed and breakfast that exuded warmth and comfort. The cosy room provided a perfect sanctuary to recharge my energy for the adventures that awaited me the following day.

Dinner called, and I ventured out into the town to sample Lichfield's culinary delights. From traditional British pubs serving hearty dishes to trendy cafes offering inventive cuisine, the town's gastronomic scene catered to all tastes and preferences. I indulged in a mouth-watering meal, savouring every bite and relishing the flavours that showcased the region's culinary prowess. The local delicacies and warm hospitality of the establishments left me with a contented heart and a smile on my face.

I returned to my cosy accommodation and couldn't help but reflect on the day's adventures. Lichfield had embraced me with its captivating beauty, rich history, and vibrant spirit. The journey had been filled with joy, discovery, and a sense of wonder. With dreams of Lichfield's enchanting streets and the promise of tomorrow's exploration dancing in my mind, I drifted off to sleep, eagerly awaiting the dawn of a new day on my A-to-Z odyssey.

LICHFIELD TO MANCHESTER

The sun peeped over the horizon, casting a warm golden glow on the picturesque town of Lichfield as I bid a fond farewell to its charming streets and embarked on the next leg of my extraordinary A-to-Z journey towards the vibrant city of Manchester. With a mixture of excitement and curiosity bubbling within me, I jumped on the train, ready to be whisked away by the enchanting landscapes and captivating experiences that awaited.

The train manoeuvred away from Lichfield Station. I settled into my seat and gazed out of the window, eager to absorb the ever-changing panorama. The Staffordshire countryside unfurled before my eyes like a watercolour painting. Rolling green hills stretched out as far as the eye could see, dotted with sheep peacefully grazing in the morning light. It was a sight that spoke of tranquillity and serenity, inviting me to unwind and embrace the natural beauty that enveloped me.

As the train journeyed further north, the landscape underwent a gradual transformation. The gentle undulations of Staffordshire's terrain gave way to the rugged grandeur of Derbyshire's Peak District. Towering peaks emerged on the horizon, their rocky façades defying the heavens above. I found myself utterly captivated by the raw beauty of nature, utterly spellbound by the sheer magnitude of the landscape that seemed to exude an ancient, mystical wisdom.

Sneaking through tunnels, the train momentarily enveloping me in darkness, only to emerge into bursts of sunlight that bathed the lush valleys and cascading waterfalls in a celestial glow. My heart danced with delight as the train traversed viaducts, suspended high above deep gorges, granting me breathtaking views that left me in awe of Mother Nature's artistry.

As the train approached Manchester, the scenery gradually shifted once again, signalling our arrival in the bustling city. The urban landscape burst into life with a vibrant energy that hummed in the air. Modern skyscrapers pierced the sky, their glass exteriors reflecting sunlight like shimmering crystals. The city's architectural diversity unfolded before me, with grand Victorian buildings standing side by side with sleek contemporary structures, creating a harmonious blend of the old and the new.

Stepping off the train at Manchester Piccadilly Station, I found myself immersed in diverse sights, sounds, and scents that stirred my senses. The city's dynamic spirit embraced me, as crowds of people hurriedly made their way through the bustling streets. The aroma of freshly brewed coffee wafted from cosy cafes, enticing me with promises of warmth and caffeinated adventures.

Eager to delve deeper into Manchester's rich history, I made my way to the iconic Manchester Town Hall. Its grand neo-Gothic architecture commanded attention, with intricate carvings, towering spires, and an imposing clock tower that seemed to reach for the heavens. Stepping inside, I marvelled at the opulent interiors, with ornate ceilings adorned with dazzling chandeliers and sweeping staircases that whispered tales of grand events and historic moments. It was a place where the past and the present converged, reminding me of the city's resilience and vibrant heritage.

Venturing further into Manchester's vibrant streets, I couldn't resist the allure of its cultural offerings. Art galleries and museums beckoned, promising an enriching exploration of creativity and human expression. The Whitworth Art Gallery, with its vast collection of contemporary and historical artworks, captured my imagination. Each brushstroke and sculpted form seemed to convey a story, inviting me to step into the artist's world and see the world through their eyes.

The day transformed into rainbow-like colours painted by the setting sun and I found myself drawn to Manchester's renowned music scene. Live music venues resonated with melodies that spilled onto the streets, enticing passers-by to stop and join the rhythm. I immersed myself in the infectious energy of the crowd, swaying to the beats and singing along with the chorus. It was a moment of pure bliss, where music united people from all walks of life, erasing boundaries and creating a shared experience of joy and togetherness.

With a satisfied appetite for art, music, and culture, I sought refuge in place called the 'Lower Turks Head' in the heart of Manchester. The elegant surroundings provided a haven of comfort, allowing me to reflect on the day's adventures. As I drifted off to sleep, I couldn't help but feel grateful for the vibrant field of experiences Manchester had woven into my journey. Tomorrow, with a renewed sense of adventure, I would set off to explore the captivating town of Norwich, eager to uncover its hidden gems and continue my tour through England's remarkable landscapes and towns.

ATLAS
ATLAS BAR
THE KNOTT

MANCHESTER TO NORWICH

The sun began to disappear behind a cluster of fluffy clouds, signalling the end of my adventure in Manchester, I bid farewell to its vibrant streets with a mixture of nostalgia and excitement. The time had come to embark on the next leg of my A-to-Z journey, and my destination was none other than the charming city of Norwich. With a spring in my step and a twinkle in my eye, I boarded the train at Manchester Piccadilly Station, ready to witness the ever-changing landscapes that awaited me.

As the train pulled away from the bustling station, the familiar sights and sounds of the city gradually faded into the distance, replaced by the peaceful embrace of the English countryside. The train snaked its way through lush meadows and rolling hills, adorned with a patchwork quilt of vibrant greens and golden yellows. It was as if Mother Nature herself had taken out her finest paintbrushes to create this picturesque scene.

With each passing mile, the landscape transformed like a whimsical painting coming to life. Quaint villages and market towns dotted the countryside, their charming facades peeping out from behind hedgerows and ancient oak trees. Each village seemed to have its own unique character, from thatched-roof cottages straight out of a storybook to colourful Georgian houses that seemed to burst with personality.

We ventured further east, the train journeyed through the counties of Cambridgeshire and Suffolk, revealing glimpses of their hidden beauty. Picturesque rivers and canals meandered through the landscape, cutting through the green fields like shimmering ribbons. I couldn't help but imagine myself punting along the tranquil waterways, a straw hat perched on my head and a contented smile on my face.

The train's rhythmic motions lulled me into a dreamlike state as we approached Norwich. The city, with its rich history and medieval charm, was like a treasure chest waiting to be opened. As the train pulled into Norwich Station, I stepped onto the platform with a sense of anticipation, ready to unlock the secrets that lay within.

The moment I set foot in Norwich; I was immediately greeted by the city's architectural wonders. Norwich Cathedral, a magnificent blend of Romanesque and Gothic styles, towered above the surrounding buildings, its intricate stone carvings telling stories of centuries past. I couldn't resist craning my neck to take in its soaring spire, feeling as though I had been transported to a bygone era of knights and damsels.

Eager to explore further, I wandered through Norwich's winding streets, where history seemed to seep from every cobblestone. Elm Hill, a street frozen in time, captured my attention with its crooked timber-framed houses and cobblestone pavement. It felt like stepping into a time capsule, a place where modern worries were left behind and the simplicity of a bygone era embraced me.

As the afternoon sun cast a warm glow over the city, I found myself irresistibly drawn to the hustle and bustle of Norwich Market. The tantalising aromas of freshly baked bread, sizzling sausages, and exotic spices wafted through the air, tempting my taste buds with their promises of culinary delights. Stalls adorned with colourful produce and artisan crafts lined the market square, each one a treasure trove waiting to be explored. I couldn't resist sampling a bit of everything, from local cheeses to delectable pastries, savouring the flavours that defined the region.

To escape the excitement of the market, I meandered along the tranquil banks of the River Wensum, which flowed gently through the heart of Norwich. The water shimmered in the late afternoon light, reflecting the majestic architecture that lined its banks. Ducks glided gracefully across the surface, their quacks and splashes adding a whimsical soundtrack to my leisurely stroll. It was a moment of pure serenity, a chance to pause and soak in the beauty of nature in the midst of an urban landscape.

As the day slowly turned into evening, I sought refuge in a cosy hotel nestled within the heart of Norwich. The warm and inviting ambiance wrapped around me like a snug blanket, offering a sanctuary to rest and recharge for the adventures that awaited me the next day. The comfortable bed beckoned, and I surrendered to its embrace, falling into a deep and restful slumber.

In the evening, my rumbling stomach led me to a local restaurant, where I indulged in the gastronomic delights of Norfolk cuisine. From succulent seafood dishes featuring freshly caught fish from the nearby coast to hearty stews bursting with local produce, every bite was a celebration of the region's culinary heritage. The flavours danced on my tongue, tantalising my taste buds and leaving me craving for more. Paired with a glass of fine Norfolk ale, the meal became a joy of taste and satisfaction.

Engaging in friendly conversations with the locals, I felt a sense of kinship and camaraderie. Their warm hospitality and lively anecdotes transformed the restaurant into a gathering place, where stories were shared, laughter echoed, and friendships bloomed. I couldn't help but feel a deeper connection to the city and its people, realising that Norwich was not just a place on the map but a community of vibrant souls.

As the night sky enveloped the city, I returned to my hotel, where a restful night's sleep awaited me. The cosy room embraced me like a warm hug, and I drifted off to sleep with a contented smile on my face, my mind filled with the memories of the day's adventures.

The next morning, as I bid farewell to Norwich, I couldn't help but feel a twinge of sadness. The city had charmed me with its rich history, architectural wonders, and welcoming spirit. But the A-to-Z journey must go on, and as I boarded the train to my next destination, the historic allure of Oxford, I carried a piece of Norwich in my heart, ready to embrace the wonders that awaited me.

As the train rolled along the tracks, carrying me away from the captivating city of Norwich and towards the historic and illustrious city of Oxford, a sense of anticipation washed over me. I couldn't help but feel a tingling in my fingertips and a fluttering in my chest, as if the very air around me crackled with excitement. Little did I know that this particular leg of my A-to-Z adventure would be filled with unexpected diversions, delightful encounters, and a healthy dose of laughter.

Leaving behind the picturesque countryside of Norfolk, the train meandered its way through the charming villages and rolling hills of Cambridgeshire. Quaint cottages with thatched roofs peeked out from behind vibrant hedges, their chimneys releasing plumes of smoke that seemed to carry with them the secrets and stories of generations past. The train's rhythmic motion lulled me into a contemplative state as I pondered the lives and experiences of those who called this idyllic landscape home.

As we ventured further along the track, the scenery changed, and I found myself gazing out at the breathtaking beauty of Suffolk. The train glided past fields of golden wheat, their whispers carried by the wind, and meandered alongside gentle rivers that sparkled like liquid silver. It was as if nature herself had painted this landscape with the brushstrokes of serenity and tranquillity.

Just when I thought the journey couldn't get any more enchanting, fate decided to inject a bit of mischief into the mix. A signal issue caused a temporary halt, and the train came to a stop, leaving us passengers in a state of mild bewilderment. But instead of frustration, a light-hearted energy filled the air, and a collective chuckle rippled through the carriage. We were all adventurers on a shared quest, and this unexpected pause was just another chapter in our grand tale.

Time seemed to stand still as we waited for the issue to be resolved, but it didn't dampen our spirits. Passengers struck up conversations with strangers, swapping tales of their own adventures and sharing insider tips about the hidden gems of Oxford. Laughter echoed through the train as impromptu games were played, and even the train staff joined in, regaling us with amusing anecdotes and tales of their own travels. It was a moment of camaraderie and connection, reminding me that the true beauty of any journey lies not only in the destination but in the people we meet along the way.

Finally, the signal issue was resolved, and the train came back to life, ready to carry us forward. As we neared Oxford, the atmosphere onboard was electric with anticipation. The train seemed to pick up speed, as if it too shared in our eagerness to explore the city's fabled streets and storied halls.

Stepping off the train in Oxford, I was immediately captivated by the city's timeless beauty. The spires of its world-renowned colleges pierced the sky, like sentinels guarding the treasures of knowledge and wisdom contained within their ancient walls. The cobbled streets beckoned me to wander, and I eagerly answered their call, my footsteps light and filled with curiosity.

Every corner turned revealed a new marvel—a hidden courtyard adorned with vibrant flowers, a centuries-old pub with a rich vein of stories etched into its walls, or a quaint bookstore where the scent of aged books mingled with the excitement of literary discovery. It was a city where history and modernity danced hand in hand, and where every street seemed to whisper secrets of the past while embracing the possibilities of the present.

As the day wore on, hunger started clawing at my stomach, reminding me that even intrepid adventurers need sustenance. I followed my nose to a cosy café tucked away on a cobblestone lane, where the aroma of freshly brewed coffee and delectable treats enveloped me like a warm embrace. The jovial atmosphere inside was infectious, with lively conversations and laughter filling the air. It was the kind of place where strangers became friends over a shared appreciation for good food and good company.

Seated with newfound companions, I relished a classic Oxfordshire specialty—the delightful Beef and Ale Pie. Tender beef, bathed in rich gravy, encased in golden pastry. The flavours danced on my tongue, a true testament to the region's culinary prowess.

As we indulged, conversation flowed effortlessly. Laughter and animated gestures punctuated our exchange. We swapped travel tales, sharing recommendations for must-visit spots in Oxfordshire. The vibrant city united us in our love for adventure and exploration.

In that charming restaurant, time seemed suspended. Our laughter resonated, creating a genuine sense of camaraderie. The shared experience of savouring the traditional dish forged connections that would endure beyond our time in Oxfordshire.

Amidst clinking glasses and culinary delights, we revelled in the magic of the moment. It was the people we met, the connections we made, and the shared experiences that truly enriched our journeys.

With the day drawing to a close, I made my way to a charming 4-star hotel called 'The Buttery' nestled in the heart of Oxford. The cosy room welcomed me like a warm hug, its soft lighting and plush furnishings creating a sanctuary of relaxation. I drifted off to sleep, a contented smile on my face, as I relished in the memories of the day's delightful diversions and unexpected encounters.

The journey from Norwich to Oxford had been a whirlwind of emotions and experiences, a testament to the unpredictable nature of travel. But amidst the diversions and delays, I had discovered the true essence of adventure—the joy of embracing the unexpected, the magic of connecting with fellow wanderers, and the sheer delight of laughter that echoed through the train carriages and along the city streets.

I closed my eyes and couldn't help but wonder what the next leg of my alphabetic adventure would bring. But one thing was certain—wherever I went and whatever challenges I encountered, I would always carry with me the spirit of light-heartedness, the zest for exploration, and the ever-present possibility of laughter.

OXFORD TO PORTSMOUTH

A fond farewell to the intellectual haven of Oxford was made as I embarked on a thrilling seaside escapade to the vibrant coastal city of Portsmouth. The anticipation of sandy shores, salty breezes, and whimsical maritime adventures filled my heart with excitement as I boarded the train at Oxford Station, ready to immerse myself in the colourful setting of this seaside gem.

The train departed, leaving behind the dreamy spires of Oxford, I gazed out of the window, captivated by the ever-changing landscapes that unfolded before me. The train rattled through the bucolic Oxfordshire countryside, where emerald-green fields stretched as far as the eye could see. Cows grazed lazily, seemingly content with their picturesque surroundings, while fluffy white sheep dotted the rolling hills like clouds in a blue sky. It was a scene straight out of a pastoral painting, and I couldn't help but marvel at the natural beauty that enveloped me.

As we ventured further south, the scenery morphed into a delightful patchwork of rural charm and urban vibrancy. Quaint villages with thatched-roof cottages emerged like colourful pops of paint on a canvas, while bustling market towns brimmed with life, their streets alive with the hustle and bustle of everyday activity. The train's rhythmic chug created a soothing backdrop as I allowed my imagination to run wild, conjuring stories of the villagers' lives and weaving tales of adventure in my mind.

Approaching Portsmouth, the train meandered closer to the coast, and a tantalising scent of salt kissed the air, hinting at the oceanic delights that awaited me. The tracks seemingly danced along the shoreline, providing glimpses of the glittering waters of the Solent and the distant silhouette of the Isle of Wight. The call of seagulls resonated in the distance, their cries a melodic tune that harmonised with the lapping waves, inviting me to join in their lively seaside chorus.

As the train glided into Portsmouth and Southsea Station, I eagerly alighted, feeling an immediate surge of energy and excitement. The maritime ambiance embraced me like a warm, salty hug. The city's rich naval history was palpable in the air, mingling with the scent of fish and chips and the lively chatter of locals and visitors alike.

Setting foot on Portsmouth's streets, I found myself immersed in a delightful blend of past and present. Historic architecture, including remnants of medieval walls and imposing fortifications, stood proudly alongside modern developments, creating a unique juxtaposition of old-world charm and contemporary vibrancy. The cobbled lanes beckoned with their timeless allure, inviting me to wander aimlessly and discover hidden gems at every turn.

The historic dockyard, a maritime treasure trove, enticed me with its promise of adventure and discovery. Excitement coursed through my veins as I explored the magnificent vessels that graced its waters. The towering masts of HMS Victory, Nelson's legendary flagship, reached towards the sky, as if proudly displaying its victorious past. The haunting remains of the Mary Rose, once lost to the depths of the Solent, now stood as a testament to the city's rich maritime heritage. I couldn't help but marvel at the ingenuity and courage of the sailors who braved the high seas aboard these majestic vessels.

Eager to immerse myself further in Portsmouth's vibrant spirit, I meandered through the city's bustling streets, drawn to the lively pubs that spilled laughter and merriment onto the cobblestones. The clinking of glasses and the infectious sounds of friendly banter welcomed me like an old friend, and I found myself drawn into conversations with locals and fellow travellers alike. Tales were spun, laughter echoed, and bonds were forged over pints of local ale, as the camaraderie of the city's residents enveloped me in its warm embrace.

With my newfound pub friends bidding me adieu, I continued my exploration, my footsteps carrying me towards the enchanting Southsea Beach. The rhythmic crashing of waves against the shore provided a soothing soundtrack as I strolled along the sun-kissed sands, relishing the feeling of warm grains beneath my feet. Families built sandcastles with laughter and determination, their creations standing tall against the whims of the tide. Kites danced in the coastal breeze, painting the sky with a kaleidoscope of colours. I revelled in the joyous atmosphere, feeling like a carefree child once more, my worries carried away by the gentle sea breeze.

As the sun began its descent, casting a warm golden glow over the city, my appetite beckoned me to one of Portsmouth's famed seafood restaurants. Nestled by the bustling harbour, the restaurant exuded a welcoming charm, its windows offering panoramic views of bobbing sailboats and fishing vessels. I settled into a cosy corner, my taste buds already tingling with anticipation.

The seafood platter that graced my table was a masterpiece of culinary delight. Succulent prawns, tender calamari, and mouth-watering fish fillets danced upon my palate, each bite a burst of flavours. The chef's mastery in combining the freshest catch with local herbs and spices was evident, and I savoured every morsel as if it were a treasure discovered in the depths of the ocean.

The restaurant staff, with their genuine warmth and hospitality, added an extra sprinkle of magic to my dining experience. They regaled me with tales of seafaring adventures and whispered secrets of the city's maritime folklore. The stories seemed to come alive, floating through the air like ethereal sea spray, painting vivid pictures in my mind and igniting my imagination.

With a satiated appetite and a heart brimming with unforgettable encounters, I made my way to a charming 4-star hotel nestled along Portsmouth's picturesque seafront. The hotel's elegant facade, adorned with flowers in full bloom, welcomed me with open arms. The attentive staff ensured every comfort was met, as if they were custodians of a magical retreat designed to rejuvenate weary adventurers. The soft embrace of the luxurious bed, paired with the gentle lullaby of crashing waves outside my window, lulled me into a deep and restful sleep, dreaming of swashbuckling adventures and seaside wonders.

As morning broke and sunlight streamed through the window, I awoke with a renewed sense of wonder and anticipation. Portsmouth had cast its spell upon me, igniting a passion for discovery and a love for the sea that would forever reside in my heart. The journey from Oxford to Portsmouth had been a full of delightful sights, sounds, and flavours, a tapestry woven with the threads of history, camaraderie, and unbridled joy.

As I prepared to bid adieu to this enchanting coastal city, I couldn't help but feel a tinge of melancholy. But as a wise sea captain once said, "The sea is a vast and endless expanse, and the world is brimming with treasures waiting to be discovered." With that thought, I set my sights on the next destination, eager to uncover the wonders that lay ahead, one letter at a time.

Emirates SPINNAKER TOWER
emirates.com

PORTSMOUTH TO QUEENBOROUGH

As I bid a fond farewell to the vibrant city of Portsmouth, my anticipation soared, knowing that my next destination was the lesser-known town of Queenborough. With a heart full of excitement and a mind brimming with curiosity, I boarded the train at Portsmouth Harbour station, ready to embark on the next chapter of my A-to-Z adventure.

Leaving behind the coastal views of Portsmouth, the train journeyed through the picturesque landscapes of Hampshire and Kent. The countryside unfolded before my eyes like a breathtaking painting. Rolling hills, adorned with vibrant greenery, stretched as far as the eye could see. Fields of golden wheat swayed gently in the breeze, creating a mesmerising dance of nature's beauty.

As we ventured deeper into Kent, the renowned Garden of England, the train passed through orchards bursting with the colours and aromas of the season. Rows of apple and cherry trees lined the countryside, their branches heavy with the promise of delicious fruits. I couldn't resist the urge to imagine myself plucking a juicy apple straight from the tree, savouring its crispness and sweetness.

The train journeyed through historic towns steeped in heritage, such as Rochester (which is a future port of call) and Sittingbourne. Majestic castles and medieval architecture whispered tales of knights and ladies, sparking my imagination and igniting a sense of wonder. I couldn't help but envision grand tournaments and noble quests unfolding in these storied settings, where the echoes of the past mingled with the present.

Crossing the Swale Estuary, a shimmering body of water that seemed to stretch on forever, the train offered panoramic views of marshlands teeming with wildlife. The air was filled with the calls of birds, creating nature's melodies. The tranquil beauty of the estuary, with its reeds swaying gently in the breeze, created a serene interlude in the journey, inviting contemplation and reflection.

Continuing onward, the train carried me across the Isle of Sheppey, revealing the island's coastal charm and small communities. Quaint seaside towns dotted the shoreline, exuding a timeless appeal. Colourful beach huts lined the promenades, adding a vibrant touch to the seaside scenery. Fishing boats bobbed in the distance, their nets casting hopeful dreams into the briny depths.

As we approached Queenborough, the train traversed the Sheerness-on-Sea Bridge, offering a sweeping vista of the River Medway and the town's picturesque setting. The train pulled into Queenborough Station, and I disembarked, ready to immerse myself in the town's historical charm and maritime allure.

Stepping onto the platform, I was greeted by a sense of tranquillity that enveloped the town. The streets, lined with quaint houses painted in an array of cheerful colours, beckoned me to explore further. The gentle murmur of the River Medway added a soothing soundtrack to my journey, as if the town itself whispered tales of its past and present.

As I wandered through the winding streets, I stumbled upon Queenborough Castle, an imposing medieval fortress perched on a hill. Its weathered stone walls stood as a testament to the town's rich history, transporting me to a time of knights and castles. I couldn't resist the urge to play the role of a valiant knight, envisioning myself defending the castle's honour against imaginary foes.

Continuing my exploration, I found myself captivated by the charm of Queenborough's independent shops and cosy cafes. Each establishment had its own distinct personality, inviting me to step inside and discover hidden treasures. The friendly locals, always ready to share a story or two, added an extra layer of warmth to my journey, making me feel like an honorary resident of this enchanting town.

Reaching Queenborough Harbour, I was greeted by a picturesque scene straight out of a postcard. Sailboats gently swayed in the harbour, their colourful sails adding a touch of whimsy to the waterfront. Seagulls soared overhead, their graceful flight painting the sky with dashes of white. It was a moment of pure serenity, where time seemed to stand still, and worries melted away.

As the sun began to set, casting a golden glow over the town, I sought solace in a charming inn nestled amidst the cobblestone streets. Its cosy rooms and welcoming staff provided a haven of comfort and quintessential British hospitality. Sitting in the inn's garden, surrounded by fragrant blooms and the cheerful banter of fellow travellers, I delighted in the flavours of the region's culinary delights, indulging in a local specialty - the exquisite Pan-Fried Sea Bass. The delicate flesh of the fish, expertly cooked to perfection, was accompanied by a medley of fresh seasonal vegetables, creating a taste that transported me to the picturesque coastal shores. With every mouthful, I celebrated the abundance of the sea and relished in the unique flavours that defined the area's gastronomic heritage. It was a moment of pure culinary bliss, immersing myself in the rich British cuisine and savouring the true essence of the region.

Under a canopy of stars, I reflected on the day's adventures, feeling grateful for the serendipity that had led me to Queenborough. This hidden gem had exceeded my expectations, offering a glimpse into the untamed beauty of England's lesser-known towns. It was a reminder that life's most extraordinary moments often lie off the beaten path, waiting to be discovered by those with a sense of adventure and an open heart.

As I drifted off to sleep, with dreams of future destinations dancing in my mind, I couldn't help but marvel at the boundless possibilities that awaited me. Queenborough had ignited a spark of curiosity and wanderlust within me, urging me to continue my letter-by-letter journey, ready to uncover the treasures that each letter held, one delightful discovery at a time.

LO13

It was a reluctant adieu to the hidden coastal gem of Queenborough, I found myself embarking on yet another train adventure, this time bound for the historic city of Rochester. With its intriguing tales of yore and its picturesque streets, Rochester promised to be a captivating destination that would unlock the mysteries of time and space.

The train journey from Queenborough to Rochester proved to be a whimsical voyage through the bucolic landscapes of Kent, renowned as the Garden of England. The undulating hills, resplendent in their vibrant green hues, unfurled before my very eyes like an artist's canvas come to life. Charming hamlets nestled amidst the countryside, boasting thatched-roof cottages and gardens brimming with an explosion of blossoms, further enhanced the idyllic ambiance.

As the train wove its way through the rural splendour, I found myself entranced by the enchanting vistas that unfurled outside my window. Fields ablaze with a kaleidoscope of wildflowers painted the panorama with their vivid hues, while docile sheep and cows meandered lazily, bestowing an air of rural serenity upon the scene. It was a veritable feast for the senses, a gathering of nature's marvels that serenaded me throughout my journey.

Eventually, the train approached Rochester, traversing the picturesque River Medway and affording me a magnificent view of the city's most iconic landmark: Rochester Castle. Standing resolute and imposing upon the riverbanks, its ancient stone walls and formidable tower stood as a testament to a bygone era of chivalry and valour. The castle's very presence stirred my imagination, conjuring visions of gallant knights and epic battles that had unfolded within its hallowed walls.

With a gentle hiss of the train, I disembarked at Rochester Station, ready to immerse myself in the labyrinthine streets steeped in history. Rochester embraced me with its timeless allure and picturesque charm, its cobbled lanes winding through deep history. The tantalising aroma of freshly baked delights wafting from quaint bakeries beckoned me further, tempting me to explore the city's hidden treasures.

Ambling along the streets, I happened upon the resplendent Rochester Cathedral, a soaring edifice of immense spiritual significance. Its intricate architecture and lofty spires spoke volumes of centuries-old devotion and masterful craftsmanship. Compelled by an irresistible force, I stepped inside the sacred sanctuary, where whispers of prayers and ethereal light streaming through stained-glass windows elevated my soul, evoking a profound sense of awe and reverence.

In my wanderings, serendipity graced me with an unexpected encounter: a lively street performance in the heart of the city. Musicians strummed mirthful melodies, while dancers twirled with abandon, their infectious laughter permeating the air. Drawn into the mirthful commotion, I found myself clapping and tapping my feet to the rhythm, swept away by the infectious jubilation that imbued the atmosphere. It was an impromptu ensemble of joy, an unplanned interlude that injected an extra dose of merriment into my Rochester sojourn.

As the sun began its descent, casting a warm, golden glow upon the city, I sought respite in a quaint riverside café. Nestled by the water's edge, I savoured a steaming cup of tea, mesmerised by the gentle current of the River Medway as it meandered past, mirroring the hues of the twilight sky. The tranquil ambiance provided the perfect backdrop for contemplation, allowing me to reflect upon the day's extraordinary encounters and cherish the simple pleasures that Rochester had bestowed upon me.

Nightfall found me nestled in a charming bed and breakfast, a hidden sanctuary tucked away in one of Rochester's quiet corners. Its snug chambers enveloped me in a warm embrace, and the sumptuous bed promised a restful night's slumber. As I succumbed to the realm of dreams, my mind conjured visions of knights and castles, gratitude filling my heart for the enchanting experiences that had enriched my Rochester sojourn.

The following morning, bidding adieu to Rochester, I carried with me a profound appreciation for its storied past, its enduring beauty, and the delightful happenstances that had rendered my visit truly extraordinary. Rochester had unveiled itself as a portal to an alternate dimension, a realm where history intertwined effortlessly with the present.

With a renewed sense of wonder and an insatiable thirst for discovery, I eagerly anticipated the next leg of my A-to-Z expedition. The path ahead teemed with anticipation, knowing that uncharted realms and concealed wonders awaited, ready to be unveiled at every twist and turn of my voyage. Rochester had left an indelible imprint upon my journey, igniting a fervour within me to embrace the unknown, to unearth the enigmatic secrets that lay shrouded in the vast expanse of this country called England.

Rochester Station

ROCHESTER TO SALISBURY

Leaving behind the rather peculiar town of Rochester, I found myself embarking on the next phase of my extraordinary journey, filled with an equal measure of excitement and bewildered curiosity. The charming city of Salisbury beckoned me with its picturesque streets and enigmatic allure, ready to unravel the secrets that lay hidden within its folds.

As I made my way to the railway station, my mind meandered through the memories I had collected thus far. Public transportation had proven to be a somewhat reliable, albeit alarmingly pricey, mode of conveyance, transporting me to realms I had only dared to dream of exploring. With a nostalgic pang and an insatiable yearning for the unknown, I boarded the train, eagerly embracing the adventures that awaited.

The train glided along the tracks away from Rochester, revealing the scenes of Kent's landscapes, a living masterpiece of rolling hills swathed in lush emerald green. Wildflowers, ablaze with vibrant hues, danced merrily in the gentle breeze, like brushstrokes of nature's artistic hand. Quaint villages, with their charming cottages nestled amidst the idyllic scenery, added a touch of rustic beauty to the tableau, reminiscent of a quaint watercolour painting.

As the train snaked its way through the countryside, I felt an overwhelming sense of tranquillity washing over me. The rhythmic clatter of the wheels echoed a soothing lullaby, lulling me into a state of peaceful contemplation. The passing fields, grazed upon by sheep and cows, exuded an air of bucolic serenity, as if time itself had decided to slow its inexorable march, granting me a fleeting respite from the frenetic pace of the modern world.

As we ventured into Surrey's embrace, the landscape underwent a metamorphosis, as if a fantastical realm unfurled its verdant canopy before my very eyes. The train navigated through leafy woodlands, where a diverse variety of flora and fauna whispered tales of ancient secrets. Golden sunlight, filtering through the interlaced branches, cast ethereal patterns upon the forest floor, evoking an irresistible sense of enchantment. I couldn't help but imagine myself as a daring explorer, venturing forth into these mystical woods in search of hidden treasures and extraordinary encounters.

As I sat mesmerised by the enchanting scenery unfolding outside the train window, my tranquillity was suddenly shattered by a heated argument that erupted a few rows ahead. An elderly gentleman, clad in a tweed jacket and sporting a well-groomed moustache, had taken offence to a teenager nonchalantly propping his feet up on the seat opposite him. The clash of generations seemed inevitable.

The elderly gentleman's voice trembled with indignation as he sternly reprimanded the young offender for his lack of manners and respect. The teenager, donning a hoodie and earphones, retorted with a dismissive shrug and muttered words that only further fuelled the flames of discord. The tension in the air grew palpable, disrupting the peaceful ambience that had enveloped the train.

Passengers turned their heads, their curiosity piqued by the escalating altercation. Murmurs of disapproval and sympathetic sighs rippled through the carriage. The clash of opinions and conflicting attitudes resonated, threatening to engulf the serene journey in chaos.

Just as it seemed that the confrontation was about to escalate into something far more volatile, the timely intervention of the ticket inspector diffused the situation. With a calm and authoritative demeanour, he stepped in, deftly navigating through the confined space to reach the heart of the conflict.

His words carried a gentle authority, reminding both parties of the importance of mutual respect and consideration. The elderly gentleman, still visibly flustered, reluctantly conceded, while the teenager, perhaps begrudgingly, withdrew his feet from the seat. The tension dissipated like a fleeting fog, leaving behind an air of uneasy calm.

Yet, the aftermath of the altercation lingered, casting a shadow over the once serene carriage. The previously engrossed passengers now wore expressions tinged with weariness and a sense of disappointment. The spell of tranquillity had been irrevocably broken, leaving an invisible rift that would take time to heal.

The argument had cast a temporary veil over the beauty that surrounded us, reminding me of the fragility of peace and the profound impact of human interactions.

However, our journey carried us through the idyllic landscapes of Wiltshire, where undulating hills and expansive fields painted a tableau of serenity and pastoral bliss. Quaint villages, their thatched-roof cottages basking in the gentle sunlight, appeared like scenes plucked straight from a storybook, inviting me to step into their nostalgic embrace and uncover their hidden treasures.

With a gentle sigh, the train glided into Salisbury Station, and I stepped onto the platform, a tingle of anticipation coursing through my veins. The city's crowning jewel, Salisbury Cathedral, loomed majestically on the horizon, its soaring spire piercing the heavens. It stood as a testament to human artistry and spiritual devotion, an emblem of the city's rich heritage and timeless grace.

As I strolled along the streets of Salisbury, a wave of enchantment washed over me. The city's timeless beauty whispered tales of bygone eras, inviting me to wander through its historic lanes and explore its hidden nooks. Intricate architectural marvels stood as silent witnesses to the passage of time, while the scent of freshly brewed coffee and the inviting ambiance of quaint cafes lured me to pause and savour the moment.

Immersing myself in Salisbury's course of history and culture, I found myself standing in awe before the grandeur of Salisbury Cathedral. Its sheer scale and intricate craftsmanship left me breathless, as if I had stumbled upon a portal to another dimension. Within its hallowed halls, a sense of tranquillity enveloped me, allowing for introspection and contemplation amidst the play of light filtering through stained-glass windows.

Yet, the allure of Salisbury extended far beyond the magnificent cathedral. Its streets, akin to a labyrinth of wonder, led me through concealed alleyways and secret gardens, unveiling pockets of enchantment tucked away from prying eyes. The bustling market square buzzed with life, where a vibrant fusion of locals and visitors converged in search of fresh produce, unique crafts, and tantalising street food. The alluring aromas that permeated the air seduced my senses, tempting me to surrender to Salisbury's gastronomic adventure.

Amidst the plethora of captivating experiences that Salisbury had to offer, I had the opportunity to embark on a guided tour to Stonehenge, an ancient and enigmatic site steeped in myth and legend. In the early evening, I joined a group of fellow explorers as we journeyed through time under the guidance of an expert. Immersed in the captivating history and fabled tales surrounding the mystical stone circle, I stood amidst the towering monoliths and felt an extraordinary connection to the past. It was as if the echoes of ancient rituals and forgotten narratives reverberated through the very essence of the land.

Although my time at Stonehenge was fleeting, it left an indelible imprint, a testament to the enduring allure and enigmatic aura of this iconic monument. As twilight descended upon Salisbury, I returned to its vibrant streets, where the echoes of ancient mysteries harmonized with the vivacity of modern life. The enchantment of the hidden alleyways, the lively market square, and the delectable culinary offerings continued to beckon, weaving an unforgettable tapestry of experiences that will forever be etched in my memory.

As twilight cast its gentle embrace over the city, I sought solace in a cosy inn nestled amidst Salisbury's tranquil streets. The warmth and hospitality of the staff welcomed me with open arms, while the comfortable accommodations provided a sanctuary of repose. From my window, I glimpsed the soft glow of streetlights casting a warm hue upon the city, creating an atmosphere of serene beauty that whispered of quiet contemplation and the mysteries of the night.

In the stillness of my room, I contemplated the financial implications of my journey thus far. Undeniably, the cost of exploration weighed heavily on my mind. However, as I reflected upon the priceless memories and personal growth that each experience had brought, I realised that the true value of travel transcends monetary concerns. The journey itself, with the mixture of encounters and revelations, enriches the soul in ways that cannot be quantified.

With a renewed sense of wonder and gratitude, I bid farewell to Salisbury, knowing that the next destination on my alphabetical odyssey would bring forth a fresh wave of discoveries and adventures. As I boarded the train, the hum of anticipation coursed through my veins, and a mischievous smile danced upon my lips. The road ahead beckoned, and I eagerly embraced the untrodden path, ready to embrace the surprises and delights that awaited me in the next chapter of my exploration of the alphabetical tour.

SALISBURY TO TELFORD

The enchanting city of Salisbury was left behind as I embarked on a train ride that would take me from the picturesque landscapes of Wiltshire to the industrial charm of Telford. As I hopped on the train at Salisbury Station, a sense of adventure filled the air, and I couldn't help but feel like a curious explorer, ready to uncover the quirks and delights of each destination along the way.

The train set off from Salisbury, and I peered out of the window, marvelling at the stunning countryside that unfolded before my eyes. The rolling hills of Wiltshire stretched out like a patchwork quilt, adorned with lush green fields and vibrant wildflowers. It was a scene straight out of a postcard, and I couldn't resist snapping a few pictures to capture the beauty of the moment.

As the train meandered through the gentle curves of the tracks, I couldn't help but be captivated by the charming villages that dotted the route. Each one seemed to have its own unique character, with thatched-roof cottages, colourful gardens, and friendly locals going about their daily lives. I imagined what it would be like to live in one of those idyllic villages, where time seemed to stand still and the pace of life was blissfully slow.

The train journeyed through Wiltshire, treating me to glimpses of historic towns that seemed frozen in time. Warminster, with its quaint market square and ancient stone buildings, exuded an old-world charm that transported me back in time. Westbury, with its towering white horse carved into the hillside, added a touch of whimsy to the journey. It was like stepping into a living history book, where the pages smelled like freshly baked scones and the ink was made of nostalgia.

As we ventured further north, the train carried me through Gloucestershire and Worcestershire, and the scenery took on a new character. The gentle hills and fertile valleys of the Cotswolds came into view, painting a picture of rural bliss. Sheep grazed peacefully in the meadows, their fluffy white coats adding a touch of serenity to the landscape. The air was filled with the sweet scent of wildflowers and the occasional chirping of birds, creating contrapuntal melodies.

But hold on tight, because the train ride had a surprise in store! As we approached the West Midlands, the scenery underwent a dramatic transformation. Suddenly, smokestacks and factories rose into the sky, giving the landscape an industrial makeover. The quaint countryside was replaced by urban sprawl, as the region's industrial might came to the forefront. It was like stepping into a time machine that transported me to the days of the Industrial Revolution, where innovation and hard work built the foundations of modern society.

Finally, the train pulled into Telford Central Station, and I disembarked. Telford welcomed me with open arms, showcasing a unique blend of old and new. The town centre was a bustling hub of activity, with shops offering everything from trendy clothes to quirky trinkets. As hunger struck, I found myself standing in front of a Greggs bakery, unable to resist the mouth-watering aroma of freshly baked goods. I indulged in their famous sausage rolls like a true connoisseur, savouring each bite and relishing in the simple pleasure of a delicious treat.

Exploring Telford's streets was like embarking on a treasure hunt. Historical landmarks intertwined with modern architecture, creating a delightful mishmash of styles. The Ironbridge Gorge stole the show with its grandeur, reminding me that Telford had played a pivotal role in the industrial revolution. The iron bridge itself stood proudly over the River Severn, as if saying, "Hey, I'm the symbol of progress, and I'm here to rock your world!"

But alas, not all adventures go according to plan. As the day wore on, I felt a rumbling in my stomach, and it wasn't just from the excitement of the journey. It turned out that my love affair with sausage rolls had consequences, and my belly wasn't too pleased with my culinary choices. I spent the rest of the evening in my bed and breakfast abode nursing a tummy ache and frequent trip to the bathroom, vowing to think twice before indulging into Greggs bakery delights.

Despite the unexpected turn of events, Telford had left an indelible mark on my journey. Its rich history, vibrant streets, and delicious pastries had brought joy to my heart and laughter to my soul. It reminded me that even the bumps along the road can become part of the story, adding a touch of humour and a lesson in moderation.

As I settled into bed that night, ready to bid Telford farewell, I couldn't help but reflect on the incredible journey I had embarked upon. From the picturesque landscapes of Wiltshire to the industrial charm of Telford, each destination had offered its own unique experiences. The A-to-Z journey had become more than just a series of train rides; it had become a treasure trove of memories and a reminder to embrace the unexpected with a light-hearted spirit.

With a renewed sense of wonder and anticipation, I eagerly awaited the next leg of my adventure, ready to discover what the journey from Telford to the familiar town of Uxbridge had in store. As the train whistle blew and the wheels started turning, I closed my eyes, knowing that the laughter, surprises, and delights of this whimsical journey would continue to shape my story.

Danger
Water H...
Children must be ...
under supervisio...

TELFORD TO UXBRIDGE

The industrious town of Telford along with most of the contents of my stomach was left behind as I embarked on a whimsical train journey that would take me from the heart of England's West Midlands to the outskirts of London. With a sense of excitement and a touch of wanderlust, I eagerly boarded the train at Telford Central Station, ready to immerse myself in the wonders that awaited me on this leg of my adventure.

As the train departed Telford, the landscape gradually transformed, bidding farewell to the urban sprawl and embracing the tranquillity of the countryside. Rolling hills and vast meadows stretched as far as the eye could see, inviting a sense of serenity and escape from the bustling city life left behind. The lush greenery enveloped me, offering a soothing balm to the weary soul.

The train journeyed through Shropshire, a county renowned for its breathtaking landscapes and picturesque villages. From charming market towns like Bridgnorth and Ludlow to the quaint hamlets nestled amidst the rolling hills, each destination revealed its own unique charm. I found myself daydreaming about idyllic country living, where time seemed to slow down and nature whispered its secrets to those who sought solace in its embrace.

As we ventured further south, the train carried me through Staffordshire, a land of rich heritage and diverse landscapes. The Staffordshire Moorlands, with their rugged beauty, provided a stunning backdrop as the train traversed the undulating terrain. I caught glimpses of historic buildings, such as the magnificent Lichfield Cathedral and the impressive Stafford Castle, standing tall and proud, testaments to the region's storied past.

Next, the train journeyed through Worcestershire, a county renowned for its picturesque countryside and charming market towns. As I gazed out the window, I was captivated by the sight of fruit orchards in bloom, their delicate blossoms painting the landscape with a burst of vibrant colours. Quaint villages with timber-framed houses dotted the route, inviting me to imagine a life steeped in tradition and community spirit.

Warwickshire, with its rolling hills and meandering rivers, welcomed me with open arms as the train continued its southward journey. The birthplace of William Shakespeare, this county was steeped in literary history and brimming with cultural landmarks. I envisioned myself strolling along the banks of the River Avon, the echo of Shakespeare's words lingering in the air, as I explored the charming town of Stratford-upon-Avon and its world-renowned theatres.

Approaching the outskirts of London, the train passed through the sprawling suburbs, a vibrant dose of diverse communities and bustling streets. The pace of life quickened, and the signs of urbanisation grew more pronounced with each passing mile. Tower blocks and row houses stood side by side, their windows reflecting the vibrant energy of the city.

As the train pulled into Uxbridge Station, I disembarked with a sense of anticipation. Uxbridge welcomed me with its blend of historic charm and modern vibrancy. The town centre beckoned with its eclectic mix of shops, cafes, and restaurants, promising a treasure trove of experiences to indulge in. I found myself wandering through the bustling streets, discovering hidden boutiques and local markets, and immersing myself in the lively atmosphere that permeated the town.

History came alive as I explored the Uxbridge Museum, housed in a magnificent Georgian building. The exhibits took me on a journey through time, unveiling the rich heritage and significant contributions that Uxbridge had made over the centuries. From its role as the headquarters of the RAF Fighter Command during World War II to its industrial legacy, the town's past unfolded before my eyes, leaving me with a profound appreciation for its place in history.

No adventure is complete without satisfying the palate, and Uxbridge's culinary scene offered a delightful array of options. From traditional British classics to global flavours, I embarked on a gastronomic journey, relishing the diverse dishes that Uxbridge had to offer.

This evening, I found myself in an Indian restaurant, immersed in the aromas of freshly ground spices. The chicken tikka masala, with its fragrant blend of spices, succulent chicken, and rich tomato-based sauce, transported me to the bustling streets of Mumbai.

Uxbridge truly catered to every culinary desire, and I relished each mouthful, immersing myself in the diverse tastes and textures that painted a vivid picture of the town's vibrant food culture.

As the day drew to a close, I found myself reflecting on the transformation that Uxbridge had undergone since my time as an employee. The town had blossomed into a thriving hub, embracing its past while embracing the future with open arms. The sense of community and warmth that permeated the streets made me feel like I was part of something greater, something that transcended time and place.

For my night's accommodation, I had secured a reservation at a rough and ready bed and breakfast pad nestled in the heart of Uxbridge. Nevertheless, once in bed and the lights out It was swarmed in darkness, the room provided me a peaceful retreat. With the drab appearance of the room well out of my mind allowing me to rest and rejuvenate before continuing my journey.

As the sun rose on a new day, I bid farewell to Uxbridge with a sense of gratitude and a heart full of memories. The town had gifted me with unforgettable experiences, both as an employee and now as a traveller. Verwood next, where new wonders and discoveries await me.

Uxbridge
LIMITED STOP
607
VMH2570
evoseti
Metroline
LA68 DWW

UXBRIDGE TO VERWOOD

The familiar streets of Uxbridge were now another memory. I embarked on the next leg of my A-to-Z journey, eagerly anticipating the enchanting town of Verwood. Little did I know that this particular journey would be filled with unexpected twists and turns, leading to a day of extraordinary encounters and unforgettable experiences.

As I settled into my seat on the train, I couldn't help but marvel at the diverse cast of characters around me. There was a group of lively tourists, armed with cameras and guidebooks, eagerly discussing their plans to explore Verwood's hidden gems. Across the aisle, a group of senior citizens engaged in a spirited game of cards, their laughter and friendly banter filling the air with a sense of camaraderie.

The train journey began smoothly, with picturesque views of the English countryside rolling past the windows. Verdant meadows stretched as far as the eye could see, dotted with grazing sheep and vibrant wildflowers. Quaint villages appeared in the distance, their thatched-roof cottages exuding charm and character.

However, as we approached Verwood, a sudden announcement disrupted the tranquil atmosphere. Due to unforeseen maintenance work on the tracks, the train would be unable to reach its final destination. Instead, we were instructed to disembark at a nearby station and continue our journey by bus.

At first, frustration lingered in the air as passengers grumbled about the inconvenience. But as we gathered at the station, a sense of camaraderie emerged. Strangers exchanged stories, shared recommendations for places to visit in Verwood, and offered reassurances that the unexpected detour would only add to the adventure.

Boarding the bus, I found myself seated next to an eccentric artist named Florence. With her vibrant attire and a mischievous twinkle in her eye, she was a walking embodiment of creativity. Florence regaled me with tales of her unconventional life, recounting her adventures across Europe and beyond. Her infectious enthusiasm and unapologetic zest for life reminded me of the beauty that lies in embracing the unexpected.

As the bus wound its way through picturesque country lanes, I couldn't help but marvel at the stunning scenery that unfolded before me. Verdant forests enveloped the landscape, their leaves glistening in the sunlight, while babbling brooks meandered alongside the road, adding a soothing soundtrack to the journey.

Finally, we arrived in Verwood, greeted by a warm and welcoming atmosphere that instantly put a smile on my face. The town centre exuded a quintessential English charm, with its quaint shops, bustling cafés, and vibrant market stalls. The air was filled with the fragrant aroma of freshly baked pastries and the melodious sound of street performers adding a lively soundtrack to the scene.

Eager to explore Verwood's treasures, I ventured into the verdant expanses of the Moors Valley Country Park. Towering trees whispered secrets as I wandered through wooded trails, stumbling upon hidden lakes and charming picnic spots. The park's adventure playground proved irresistible, and I couldn't resist indulging my inner child by climbing through rope ladders and whizzing down exhilarating slides.

As the day turned into evening, I found myself in an inviting pub for the night, where laughter and lively conversations filled the air. Locals and tourists mingled effortlessly, sharing stories and raising glasses in celebration of Verwood's warm hospitality. The pub's cosy ambiance and friendly atmosphere made it the perfect place to unwind, exchanging tales of the day's adventures and making connections that would last a lifetime. This is where I stayed overnight as they offered me a bed for the night as a reasonable price.

Reflecting on the day's events, I couldn't help but marvel at how the unexpected detour had transformed the journey into remarkable encounters and discoveries. The detour had brought me Florence, the colourful artist, and introduced me to Verwood's breathtaking landscapes and vibrant community.

After a hearty pub breakfast, I bid farewell to Verwood, I carried with me not only the memories of a town filled with charm and beauty but also a reminder of the beauty that lies in embracing the unexpected. The adventure had taken an unexpected turn, and I eagerly looked forward to the next destination on my journey—a town that promised to be equally enchanting, filled with its own unique surprises and wonders.

VERWOOD TO WINCHESTER

Leaving behind the peaceful village of Verwood, I embarked on a journey that would take me through winding roads and verdant landscapes, leading me to the historic and captivating city of Winchester. As I boarded the bus, excitement coursed through my veins, and I eagerly settled into my seat, ready to immerse myself in the sights and sounds of this vibrant destination.

The bus pulled away from Verwood, bidding farewell to the quaint cottages and idyllic countryside. The road stretched out before us, lined with towering trees that seemed to whisper secrets to the passing travellers. The gentle hum of conversation filled the bus, as fellow adventurers chatted and shared stories of their own explorations.

The journey to Winchester was a feast for the eyes. Rolling hills swathed in emerald green unfolded like a patchwork quilt, dotted with grazing sheep and blossoming wildflowers. The air carried a sweet scent, infused with the essence of nature. I couldn't help but gaze out the window, mesmerised by the changing landscape and the ever-present sense of tranquillity that enveloped me.

As the bus meandered along the winding roads, we passed through picturesque villages that seemed frozen in time. Quaint thatched-roof cottages adorned with vibrant flower gardens beckoned from the roadside, their charm captivating my imagination. I imagined the stories that lay hidden within those ancient walls, tales of love, laughter, and the passage of time.

Approaching Winchester, the scenery transitioned, revealing glimpses of the city's vibrant urban life. The bus glided past bustling markets, where locals and visitors intermingled, sampling fragrant spices, browsing through stalls adorned with handmade crafts, and savouring the flavours of the region. The lively atmosphere was infectious, and I couldn't resist stepping off the bus to join in the festivities.

Eager to delve deeper into Winchester's rich history, I made my way to the crown jewel of the city—the majestic Winchester Cathedral. Its towering spires reached for the heavens, an architectural marvel that stood as a testament to human ingenuity and devotion. As I stepped inside, a hush fell over me, and I found myself humbled by the grandeur and spiritual aura that filled the sacred space. The stained-glass windows painted ethereal scenes, casting colourful rays of light that danced across the stone walls, as if whispering tales of centuries gone by.

Leaving the cathedral, I embarked on a voyage of discovery through Winchester's labyrinthine streets. The city's historical heritage was evident at every turn, with timber-framed buildings leaning precariously against each other, and narrow cobbled lanes leading me on an enchanting journey through time. Quaint shops, brimming with antiques, books, and curiosities, beckoned me to explore their treasures, while inviting cafes offered respite and the chance to savour a steaming cup of tea or a delectable slice of cake.

I meandered through the city's verdant parks, where the scent of freshly cut grass mingled with the melodies of chirping birds. The River Itchen, a ribbon of serenity, flowed gracefully through the city, inviting me to stroll along its banks and lose myself in contemplation. I watched as swans glided across the water, their graceful movements mirroring the tranquillity that enveloped Winchester.

As the day drew to a close, I found myself in a cosy pub, where laughter and lively conversation filled the air. The locals regaled me with tales of Winchester's colourful past, sharing legends and anecdotes that added a touch of magic to my visit. With a pint in hand and a smile on my face,

I revelled in the camaraderie and warmth that permeated the pub, feeling like an honorary Winchester resident.

Retiring to my comfortable accommodation, a 2-star hotel nestled amidst the city's charming streets, during my meal there, I reflected on the day's journey. Winchester had spellbound me with its rich history, architectural marvels, and enchanting atmosphere. It was a city that effortlessly blended the past and the present, embracing tradition while embracing the vibrancy of modern life.

As I drifted off to sleep, dreams of Winchester danced in my mind. Images of majestic cathedrals, winding streets, and the laughter of newfound friends filled my imagination. With a heart full of gratitude and anticipation, I eagerly awaited the next step of my tour—a journey to the captivating town of Exeter, where new wonders and unforgettable experiences awaited me.

CITY MUSEUM
DISCOVER

WINCHESTER TO (E)XETER

With Winchester fading into the distance, I found myself on a train bound for Exeter, a city brimming with promise and unknown wonders. The excitement tingled in the air as I settled into my seat, eager to uncover the treasures that awaited me in this southwestern gem.

As the train departed Winchester, the landscape transformed before my eyes. The lush, green fields and rolling hills of Hampshire gradually gave way to a more rugged and coastal terrain. The train meandered through picturesque villages and charming towns, offering tantalising glimpses of thatched-roof cottages, blooming gardens, and quaint village pubs. The countryside unfolded like a patchwork quilt; each scene more captivating than the last.

As we ventured deeper into Devon, the scenery became even more enchanting. The train hugged the coastline, revealing breathtaking vistas of towering cliffs and golden beaches. The rhythmic sound of crashing waves accompanied us, beckoning me to explore the sandy shores and dip my toes in the refreshing waters. The allure of seaside resorts dotted along the coast tempted me with promises of sun-soaked adventures and coastal charm.

Passing through vibrant towns and historic landmarks, I marvelled at the architectural wonders that lined our route. Elegant Georgian buildings stood proudly alongside half-timbered houses, each telling a tale of the city's rich history. The train journey became a feast for the eyes, as if travelling through a living museum where the past seamlessly intertwined with the present.

As the train approached Exeter, my heart quickened with anticipation. The city's skyline came into view, dominated by the spires of Exeter

Cathedral—a majestic sight that stirred a sense of reverence within me. I couldn't wait to explore the narrow streets, immerse myself in the city's vibrant atmosphere, and uncover the hidden gems that lay nestled within its historic walls.

Stepping off the train at Exeter St Davids Station, I took a deep breath, ready to embark on my Exeter escapade. The city welcomed me with open arms, and I immediately felt a sense of warmth and hospitality emanating from its streets.

My first stop was Exeter Cathedral, an architectural marvel that stood as a testament to the city's storied past. As I entered the grand cathedral, I was greeted by a sense of tranquillity. Sunlight filtered through stained glass windows, casting a kaleidoscope of colours upon the ancient stone floors. I marvelled at the intricate carvings and awe-inspiring architecture, losing myself in the magnificence of this sacred space.

Leaving the cathedral behind, I ventured into the heart of the city, where a labyrinth of winding streets awaited. Each corner turned revealed a new discovery—quaint shops, charming cafes, and bustling markets. The vibrant energy of the city was infectious, as locals and visitors alike meandered through the bustling streets, savouring the unique blend of history and modernity that Exeter offered.

Hungry from my adventures, I followed my nose to the bustling Quayside, a vibrant hub of culinary delights. The tantalising aromas of freshly caught seafood and local delicacies filled the air, leading me to an array of riverside restaurants and food stalls. I couldn't resist sampling the local specialties, indulging in creamy Devonshire clotted cream, freshly baked pasties, and delectable artisan chocolates. Each bite was a celebration of Exeter's gastronomic prowess, leaving my taste buds dancing with delight.

Rejuvenated and with a skip in my step, I continued my exploration, weaving through the city's rich history and culture. I stumbled upon hidden courtyards and stumbled upon historic landmarks, each revealing a different chapter in Exeter's captivating story. From the remains of its Roman walls to the medieval charm of the Guildhall, every step deepened my appreciation for the city's heritage.

As the day drew to a close, I found myself in a cosy pub, surrounded by a diversity of faces and conversations. Some locals welcomed me, sharing stories. With a pint in hand accompanied with some pub food, namely egg, bacon, ships and sausages, I toasted to the spirit of Exeter and the unforgettable experiences it had bestowed upon me.

Exhausted but filled with food and beer and a sense of complete contentment, I made my way, the best I could in a straight line, to my accommodations—a charming bed and breakfast that exuded warmth and comfort. It was nestled in a quiet corner of the city and provided the perfect sanctuary to reflect on the day's adventures and to recharge for the journey ahead.

As I lay in bed, the memories of Exeter danced through my mind. The picturesque landscapes, the historic treasures, and the warm-hearted people all left an indelible mark on my soul. With a sense of gratitude and excitement, I drifted off to sleep, eager to continue my trip which was nearing the end, but yet still more wonders waiting to be explored.

(E)XETER TO YORK

As I boarded the train at Exeter St Davids Station, little did I know that my journey to York would hold a delightful surprise from the past. With a heart full of anticipation, I settled into my seat, ready to embrace the adventure that lay ahead.

As the train clickety-clacked along, the picturesque landscapes of Devon gradually gave way to the charming countryside of Somerset and Gloucestershire. Rolling hills, dotted with grazing sheep, and quaint villages with their thatched-roof cottages painted a serene backdrop for my journey. It was as if I had stepped into a postcard, immersing myself in the beauty of rural England.

As we ventured further north, the train journeyed through the Midlands, crossing Worcestershire and Staffordshire. The landscape transformed once again, revealing sprawling farmlands and picturesque market towns. I couldn't help but marvel at the quaint beauty that surrounded me, feeling a sense of appreciation for the simplicity and charm of these lesser-explored regions.

The train continued its steady progression, finally entering the realm of North Yorkshire. The scenery underwent a dramatic change, as the train journeyed through the breathtaking valleys and undulating moorlands of the Yorkshire Dales. The rugged beauty of the landscape, with its heather-covered hills and picturesque stone walls, captured my imagination and stirred a sense of adventure within me.

At long last, the train arrived at York Station, and I stepped off in careful mode to mind the gap. Little did I know that an unexpected reunion awaited me amidst the ancient streets of this historic city.

As I roamed the familiar cobbled lanes of York, reminiscing about my university days, fate intervened and reunited me with an old friend from that cherished chapter of my life. Amidst the bustling crowd, I caught a glimpse of a familiar face, and my heart skipped a beat. There, standing before me, was my long-lost companion, someone I hadn't seen in years.

Excitement and nostalgia washed over us as we embraced, recounting tales of our youthful escapades and shared experiences. It felt like time had stood still, and we were transported back to our carefree days of university. With joyful laughter and a twinkle in our eyes, we decided to spend the evening together, reliving the adventures of our youth.

We sought out a familiar tranquil pub tucked away in a quiet corner of the city, where the ambiance was perfect for reminiscing and letting our inhibitions loosen, just as we used to. With pints of local ale in hand, we exchanged stories, reliving the laughter, the camaraderie, and the occasional mischief that had characterised our university days.

As the evening wore on, we found ourselves slipping into that familiar rhythm of shared memories and light-hearted banter. We laughed uproariously, raised our glasses in nostalgic toasts, and recreated inside jokes that only we could fully understand. It was as if the years melted away, and we were transported back to a time when responsibilities were far from our minds.

As the night progressed, our laughter grew louder, and the stories became more animated. We shared anecdotes that had been tucked away in the corners of our minds, bringing them to life once again. The pub became a sanctuary, shielding us from the outside world, as we basked in the warmth of old friendships and the comfort of shared history.

We revelled in the freedom of the evening, allowing ourselves to get a little carried away with the merriment. The worries and stresses of adulthood faded into the background as we embraced the carefree spirit of our younger selves. It was a night of uninhibited joy, where the bonds of friendship were reignited and celebrated in all their glory.

As the night drew to a close, we bid each other farewell, promising to keep in touch and vowing not to let another moment of our lives slip away without reconnecting. The encounter had reminded us of the enduring bonds forged in our youth, and we pledged to make more time for the friendships that had shaped us into who we were today.

The next day, with a slightly heavy head (for the second night running) and a heart full of cherished memories, I bid farewell to York. The city had been the backdrop for a truly memorable reunion, reminding me of the power of old friendships and the beauty of shared experiences. As the train pulled away from the station, I couldn't help but feel a profound sense of gratitude for the unexpected twists and turns that life had brought my way.

With newfound appreciation for the journey, I eagerly looked ahead to the next stop on my A-to-Z tour. The Nottinghamshire village of Zouch beckoned, promising new encounters and experiences. Each leg of my journey continued to unfold like an array of cherished moments, weaving together the threads of past and present into a vibrant tableau of life's extraordinary surprises.

YORK TO ZOUCH

The cherished memories of York still danced vividly in my mind as I embarked on a new chapter of my adventure, setting my sights on the picturesque village of Zouch. Nestled amidst the rolling hills and verdant countryside, this hidden gem beckoned me with promises of a destination untouched by time. Little did I know that this leg of the journey would prove to be the longest and most adventurous yet, with no direct routes viable to reach my final destination.

With my trusty backpack securely fastened and a curious spirit pulsing through my veins, I was ready to embrace the unknown and uncover the hidden gems that lay along the meandering path to Zouch. The early morning sun cast a golden hue over the historic streets of York as I made my way to the bustling York Bus Station. The air was thick with anticipation, an electric buzz of excitement emanating from the travellers embarking on their own journeys, each with their own destination etched in their hearts. I joined the queue, ticket in hand, eagerly waiting to board the coach that would transport me closer to the enchanted village.

As the coach rumbled to a halt, I found myself a comfortable seat by the window, a coveted vantage point from which I could witness the landscapes unfurling before my eager eyes. The journey from York to Nottingham began, and we glided through the gentle undulations of the Yorkshire countryside. Rolling hills, dressed in a patchwork quilt of emerald green, dotted with sheep that grazed lazily in the sunshine, greeted me at every turn. It was a scene straight out of a postcard, a picturesque display of nature's beauty.

Time seemed to bend and twist, as if caught in the whims of a mischievous fairy, as I sat transfixed by the ever-changing views outside my window. The coach journey became a melange of moments -

moments of quiet reflection as I allowed the sights to seep into my soul, and moments of engaging conversation with fellow passengers. We swapped tales of past travels, shared laughter that echoed through the aisles, and occasionally whispered recommendations for must-see attractions along the way. It was as if we formed a temporary community, connected by the shared experience of exploration.

After a couple of hours that passed in what felt like the blink of an eye, we arrived at the bustling Nottingham Coach Station. Stepping off the coach, I was enveloped by a whirlwind of activity. The station thrived with a vibrant energy as travellers scurried to catch their connections, eager to continue their own adventures. In this brief interlude before my next leg, I took the opportunity to stretch my legs and refuel with a quick snack from a nearby café. The aroma of freshly brewed coffee and the tantalising scent of pastries wafted through the air, mingling with a sober chat with a local business man. It was a moment of respite amidst the flurry of movement, a chance to recharge before the next stage of my journey.

With a satisfied appetite and a renewed sense of anticipation, I boarded the next bus that would carry me closer to Zouch. As the engine roared to life, we ventured further into the heart of the English countryside, navigating the winding country lanes that painted an idyllic picture of rural life. I watched in awe as the landscape unfolded like a living embroidery, weaving a story of bucolic beauty. Verdant fields stretched as far as the eye could see, kissed by the warm embrace of sunlight, while charming villages emerged from the embrace of the rolling hills like miniaturised havens of tranquillity. The trees stood tall and proud, their branches swaying in harmony with the gentle breeze, whispering secrets of the land they called home. It was a journey that allowed me to truly appreciate the captivating allure and serenity of rural England, an escape from the cacophony of modern life.

As the bus gradually neared my destination, a flutter of excitement stirred within my chest. Zouch awaited me, a place shrouded in mystery and enchantment, its name alone evoking a sense of wonder. Finally, the moment arrived as the bus came to a gentle halt. I stepped off, my feet meeting the solid ground of Zouch, ready to immerse myself in the charm and tranquillity of this hidden village.

Zouch greeted me with open arms, embracing me in its quaint charm and peaceful ambience. The village seemed to have been plucked from the pages of a storybook, its streets adorned with thatched-roof cottages that stood as sentinels of a bygone era. Colourful gardens bloomed with a riot of flowers, adding a touch of vibrancy to the tranquil surroundings. The air was infused with the soothing scents of nature, and the melodic chirping of birds provided a concert to accompany my explorations.

Armed with a map and a spirit of adventure, I embarked on a leisurely stroll through Zouch's narrow lanes. Each twist and turn revealed new wonders, charming tea rooms where locals gathered for a cup of afternoon tea, and boutique shops that showcased handmade crafts crafted by the skilled hands of talented artisans. It was a whimsical journey, where every corner turned held the promise of discovery.

One of the highlights of my visit was stumbling upon a hidden gem nestled amidst the heart of Zouch – a centuries-old church steeped in history. Its weathered stones stood as a testament to the passage of time, adorned with intricate stonework that told stories of days long past. As I stepped inside, the peaceful ambience enveloped me like a warm embrace. The hushed silence invited contemplation and reflection, allowing me to connect with the rich heritage of the village and the lives of its past inhabitants. It was a sacred space, where history whispered in a language only the heart could understand.

As the day gracefully unfolded, I couldn't help but feel a deep sense of appreciation for the beauty and serenity that Zouch offered. Unlike bustling city streets, this village moved to its own rhythm, unburdened by the frenetic pace of modern life. The absence of crowds and tourist attractions allowed me to immerse myself fully in the authentic picture of village life. Warm greetings were exchanged with the friendly locals I encountered along the way, and their genuine hospitality left an indelible mark on my heart. It was as if I had stumbled upon a hidden community, a haven of kindness and connection.

With the day gently descending into twilight, I sought respite in a cosy bed and breakfast nestled amidst Zouch's tranquil surroundings. The warmth of the accommodation and the genuine hospitality of the hosts provided the perfect sanctuary for a peaceful night's rest. The soft embrace of fresh linen and the whispers of a quiet night lulled me into a deep slumber, my dreams infused with the sights and sounds of Zouch.

As the first rays of morning light painted the sky, I bid farewell to Zouch, carrying with me the memories of its quaint beauty and the warmth of its welcoming residents. This journey from York to Zouch had been an epic, but delightful detour, a captivating escape from the hustle and bustle of daily life. It had allowed me to slow down, to immerse myself in the simplicity and charm of village living.

With renewed energy and a sense of wanderlust still dancing in my heart, I eagerly embarked on the final leg of my A-to-Z expedition – the journey back home. As I retraced my steps, my mind overflowed with extraordinary adventures And so, with a contented smile I bid adieu to Zouch, setting my sights on the horizon of home in Bulgaria once more, my mind full of memories that will never be deleted.

Reflecting

Embarking on the A-to-Z tour of England, I set out on a whirlwind adventure through picturesque towns, historic cities, and charming villages that had come randomly out of a hat. From the quaint streets of Amersham to the vibrant energy of York, each destination had its own unique story to tell.

I navigated the intricate web of public transport, hopping on and off trains, buses, and trams to reach my destinations. Along the way, I marvelled at the scenic countryside, witnessed architectural wonders, and engaged in conversations with locals, uncovering the heart and soul of each place.

In Bath, I immersed myself in Roman history, strolling through the grandeur of the Roman Baths and marvelling at the iconic Royal Crescent. Cambridge captivated me with its rich academic heritage, showcasing the breath-taking beauty of its historic colleges and serene punting on the river Cam.

I ventured through the bustling streets of Manchester, where the spirit of music and football intertwined, before winding my way to the historic city of Norwich, with its magnificent cathedral and medieval charm. Oxford, steeped in scholarly prestige, delighted me with its magnificent colleges and captivating Bodleian Library.

Exploring Portsmouth, I delved into maritime history, discovering the iconic HMS Victory and exploring the historic dockyard. Winchester's ancient streets and grand cathedral transported me back in time, while the vibrant city of York welcomed me with its medieval walls and bustling Shambles.

Journeying from Telford to Uxbridge, I rediscovered familiar places with fresh eyes, appreciating their unique charms as a tourist. Along the way, I encountered delays, met an old friend, and even experienced a bout of sickness, reminding me that adventures often come with unexpected twists.

In each destination, I savoured the local flavours, from traditional cream teas in Exeter to indulgent homemade fish and chips. I chatted with friendly locals, soaked in the vibrant atmosphere of bustling markets, and relished/ the warm hospitality that made me feel at home wherever I went.

As I reached the final leg of my journey, I arrived at the tranquil village of Zouch, a place I had never heard of before. The journey had taken me through 26 destinations chosen randomly, from well-known cities to hidden gems, revealing the diverse beauty and captivating stories of England.

The A-to-Z tour was not just about ticking off names on a map; it was about immersing myself in the rich English culture, history, and landscapes. It was about forging connections with people, experiencing the rhythm of each place, and creating lifelong memories.

As I reflected on the adventures and experiences encountered on the tour, I realised that England has treasures in every corner. From the scenic countryside to the vibrant cities, from historic landmarks to unexpected encounters, the A-to-Z journey had woven together unforgettable moments, painting a vivid picture of diversity, beauty and charm that England has to offer.

The Budget

I meticulously planned my A-Z tour of England, excited to explore the rich history, picturesque landscapes, and vibrant cities. With a budget of £6000, I carefully allocated funds for various expenses.

Travelling expenses: To make the most of my journey, I decided to rely on trains, buses, and trams as my primary modes of transport, immersing myself in the local public transport network. I estimated that the combined cost of tickets for intercity train journeys, local buses, and trams would amount to around £1200.

Overnight stays: I aimed for a mix of accommodations to experience different aspects of English culture. I planned to spend several nights in affordable bed and breakfast establishments in charming villages, where public transport connections were easily accessible. Additionally, I included some budget-friendly hotels in major cities. Considering an average cost of £100 per night, I estimated that accommodation would amount to £2600.

Daily expenses: Being a food enthusiast, I was eager to sample local cuisines and indulge in culinary delights. I set aside a budget of £30 per day for meals and snacks, estimating that it would add up to £780 for the duration of my trip. Additionally, I allotted £400 for entrance fees to various attractions, including historic sites, museums, and iconic landmarks.

With these estimations, I was confident that my total expenses would fall within my initial budget of £6000.

During my journey, I adhered to my plan of relying mainly on trains, buses, and trams for transportation. However, there were a couple of instances where I found it more convenient to use a taxi due to unique circumstances, such as reaching my night's lodging having limited time or facility with public transport. These two taxi rides amounted to an additional £50.

Despite these minor adjustments, the majority of my travel expenses aligned with my initial estimates. My accommodation costs remained at £2600, and my daily expenses for food and attractions stayed within the allocated budget of £780 and £400, respectively.

Combined with minor miscellaneous expenses, such as souvenirs and unexpected local events, the final tally for my A-Z tour of England amounted to approximately £6230. (Not including the flights and transfers from Bulgaria before and after the tour.)

I was pleased that my careful planning and preference for utilising trains, buses, and trams as my primary modes of transport helped me stay within my budget. The journey was filled with memorable experiences, breathtaking sights, and the joy of discovering England's hidden gems. It served as a testament to the convenience and charm of public transportation, and I was grateful for the opportunity to explore the country while keeping my expenses in check.

About the Author

Martin Miller-Yianni, born in Erith, Kent in 1958, is a versatile and passionate author who embarked on his writing journey after the age of 50. His exploration of the power of words to create immersive experiences has led him to craft a unique and captivating account of his A-to-Z tour of England using public transport from notes made in 2019.

Before becoming an author, Martin had a diverse background. He worked as a primary school teacher and later as a peripatetic teacher, offering support to learners with special needs. However, it was his move to Bulgaria in 2005 that sparked his interest in writing. Despite lacking formal training, Martin's dedication and natural storytelling ability quickly propelled him into the literary world.

Martin's writing style is characterised by its honesty and meticulous attention to detail. With each page, he invites readers to join him on an extraordinary journey through England, relying solely on public transport. Through vivid descriptions and relatable characters, he captures the essence of each destination and the people he encounters along the way.

His book chronicles his A-to-Z tour, offering readers an intimate glimpse into the rich diversity of England's landscapes, history, and culture. From bustling cityscapes to quaint countryside villages, Martin's storytelling immerses readers in the beauty and charm of each location.

With a keen eye for observation and a genuine passion for storytelling, Martin paints a vivid picture of his experiences during the tour. His words not only entertain but also inspire readers to appreciate the wonders that can be discovered through public transport and the connections made with fellow travellers.

Through his work, Martin aims to provoke thought and leave readers with a deeper understanding of the human experience. His book is a testament to his unwavering dedication to crafting engaging narratives that resonate with readers, inviting them to embark on their own adventures, whether in their imagination or in real life.

9 786197 742046